Publishing

GW00544042

LEVEL by LEVEL

MATHEMATICS
National Curriculum

LEVEL
7

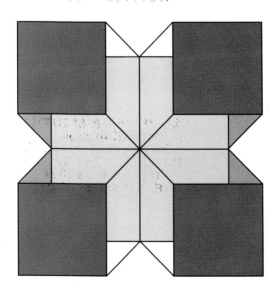

EHC Publishing
Bradford on Avon • London

INTRODUCTION

The *Level by Level Mathematics National Curriculum CHECKERS* scheme comprises student books of tests and accompanying Teacher's Guides covering the whole of the Programmes of Study and Level Description content for each Level of the (Dearing) National Curriculum. The material can be used to provide assessment for any Mathematics National Curriculum teaching scheme or text book course.

There is student material and a Teacher's Guide for each National Curriculum Level.

This is a student book for **Level 7**.

Supported by *Level by Level PoS Mathematics* (see opposite), the scheme provides a comprehensive course of National Curriculum learning material and assessment for each National Curriculum Level.

For full details of the structure of the tests, see the Teacher's Guide.

Published by

EHC Publishing
PO Box 1780
Bradford on Avon
Wilts
BA15 1YD

Tel: 01225 862879
Fax: 01225 863337

© EHC Publishing 1996

First Published 1996

Printed in Great Britain by Tadberry Evedale Ltd, London

Set in Helvetica

ISBN 1-872936-73-3

NOTES AND GUIDANCE

1. Content

There are *two* tests, CHECKER A and CHECKER B for *each* Programmes of Study *unit* (PoS) and Level Description *component* (LD) at Level 7 [see the Contents list, pages (ii) - (iv), for a full list of tests].

2. Using the tests

(See the Teacher's Guide for full details and answers.)

To test attainment on **Programmes of Study units***:* Use tests marked PoS, and PoS/LD (miss out the tests marked LD only).

To test attainment on **Level Description components***:* Use tests marked LD, and PoS/LD - the tests with grey patches at the heading (miss out the tests marked PoS only).

To test attainment on **Programmes of Study units** and **Level Description components***:* Use all tests.

3. Scoring the tests and recording attainment

Attainment can be recorded on the Record Grid, pages (v) - (vi), if individual students are retaining this book for their own use.

If sets of books are kept as class copies and handed out to students at appropriate times for testing, the grid in the Teacher's Guide can be copied and completed for each individual student.

There are five two part questions in each test. Marks can therefore be given out of 10 for each test. Teachers will prefer to determine their own criteria for success on a particular test and to develop and refine this with experience, according to the intended use - for SATS prediction, reporting to parents, group and Year Group comparisons, end of year tests, diagnosing strengths and weaknesses, assessing performance on Programmes of Study content, and so on. A useful starting point for predicting SATS performance, however, might be to consider a score of 5 or more to indicate an acceptable performance on both Programmes of Study tests and Level Description component tests. This roughly accords with SATS criteria in which students normally have to answer one item correctly out of 2 to be considered to have achieved at a particular Level, although it should be remembered that the tests here are much more extensive than those of the SATS.

4. Classroom learning material

The EHC series *Level by Level PoS Mathematics* complements *Level by Level Mathematics National Curriculum CHECKERS*. The student books for *Level by Level PoS Mathematics* provide Programmes of Study classroom work with content ordered in the same way as *Level by Level Mathematics National Curriculum CHECKERS*. Teachers using other main courses will be able to identify the relevant Programmes of Study units and Level Description components in their own course books and use *Level by Level Mathematics National Curriculum CHECKERS* with equal success.

CONTENTS

Key: LD1, LD2, ... are the components of the Dearing/SCAA Level Descriptions for each Attainment Target.
PoS1, PoS2, ... are the Programmes of Study units devised for each Level Description component.
(PoS) is a Programmes of Study *unit* test.
(LD) is a Level Description *component* test.
(PoS/LD) tests both a Programmes of Study *unit* and a Level Description *component*.

Ma1 Using and Applying Mathematics

LD1 Starting from problems or contexts that have been presented to them, pupils introduce questions of their own which generate fuller solutions.
    PoS1 ASKING QUESTIONS
        CHECKER A (PoS/LD)   1
        CHECKER B (PoS/LD)   2

LD2 They examine critically and justify their choice of mathematical presentation, considering alternative approaches and explaining improvements they have made.
    PoS1 MAKING IMPROVEMENTS
        CHECKER A (PoS/LD)   3
        CHECKER B (PoS/LD)   4

LD3 Pupils justify their generalisations or solutions, showing some insight into the mathematical structure of the situation being investigated.
    PoS1 EXPLAINING SOLUTIONS
        CHECKER A (PoS/LD)   5
        CHECKER B (PoS/LD)   6

LD4 They appreciate the difference between mathematical explanation and experimental evidence.
    PoS1 EXPLANATION AND EVIDENCE
        CHECKER A (PoS/LD)   7
        CHECKER B (PoS/LD)   8

Ma2 Number and Algebra

LD1 In making estimates, pupils round to one significant figure and multiply and divide mentally.
    PoS1 MENTAL ESTIMATES
        CHECKER A (PoS/LD)   9
        CHECKER B (PoS/LD)   10

LD2 They understand the effects of multiplying and dividing by numbers between 0 and 1.
    PoS1 MULTIPLYING AND DIVIDING BY NUMBERS LESS THAN 1
        CHECKER A (PoS/LD)   11
        CHECKER B (PoS/LD)   12

LD3 Pupils solve numerical problems involving multiplication and division with numbers of any size, using a calculator efficiently and appropriately.
    PoS1 USING CALCULATOR MEMORY
        CHECKER A (PoS)   13
        CHECKER B (PoS)   14
    PoS2 USING CALCULATOR BRACKETS
        CHECKER A (PoS)   15
        CHECKER B (PoS)   16
    PoS3 SOLVING PROBLEMS
        CHECKER A (PoS/LD)   17
        CHECKER B (PoS/LD)   18

LD4 They understand and use proportional changes.
    PoS1 PROPORTIONAL AMOUNTS
        CHECKER A (PoS/LD)   19
        CHECKER B (PoS/LD)   20

LD5 Pupils find and describe in symbols the next term or nth term of a sequence where the rule is quadratic.
    PoS1 RULES FOR SEQUENCES
        CHECKER A (PoS)   21
        CHECKER B (PoS)   22
    PoS2 QUADRATIC RULES AND EXPRESSIONS
        CHECKER A (PoS)   23
        CHECKER B (PoS)   24
    PoS3 QUADRATIC RULES FOR SEQUENCES
        CHECKER A (PoS/LD)   25
        CHECKER B (PoS/LD)   26

LD6 Pupils use graphical methods to solve simultaneous linear equations in two variables.
    PoS1 SOLVING SIMULTANEOUS EQUATIONS: USING GRAPHS
        CHECKER A (PoS/LD)   27
        CHECKER B (PoS/LD)   28

LD7 Pupils use algebraic methods to solve simultaneous linear equations in two variables.
    PoS1   SOLVING SIMULTANEOUS EQUATIONS
             CHECKER A (PoS/LD)   29
             CHECKER B (PoS/LD)   30

LD8 They solve simple inequalities.
    PoS1   INEQUALITY STATEMENTS
             CHECKER A (PoS)   31
             CHECKER B (PoS)   32
    PoS2   SOLVING INEQUALITIES
             CHECKER A (PoS/LD)   33
             CHECKER B (PoS/LD)   34

Ma3 Shape, Space and Measures

LD1 Pupils understand and apply Pythagoras' theorem when solving problems in two dimensions.
    PoS1   PYTHAGORAS' RULE
             CHECKER A (PoS)   35
             CHECKER B (PoS)   36
    PoS2   USING PYTHAGORAS' RULE
             CHECKER A (PoS/LD)   37
             CHECKER B (PoS/LD)   38

LD2 They calculate lengths, areas and volumes in plane shapes and right prisms.
    PoS1   CALCULATING LENGTHS AND AREAS
             CHECKER A (PoS)   39
             CHECKER B (PoS)   40
    PoS2   VOLUMES OF PRISMS
             CHECKER A (PoS)   41
             CHECKER B (PoS)   42
    PoS1-2 LENGTH, AREA AND VOLUME
             CHECKER A (LD)   43
             CHECKER B (LD)   44

LD3 Pupils enlarge shapes by a fractional scale factor.
    PoS1   ENLARGING SHAPES
             CHECKER A (PoS/LD)   45
             CHECKER B (PoS/LD)   46

LD4 They determine the locus of an object moving according to a rule.
    PoS1   LOCUS
             CHECKER A (PoS/LD)   47
             CHECKER B (PoS/LD)   48

LD5 Pupils appreciate the continuous nature of measurement and recognise that a measurement given to
     the nearest whole number may be inaccurate by up to one half in either direction.
    PoS1   ACCURACY IN MEASUREMENTS
             CHECKER A (PoS/LD)   49
             CHECKER B (PoS/LD)   50

LD6 They understand and use compound measures, such as speed.
    PoS1   DISTANCE, SPEED AND TIME
             CHECKER A (PoS)   51
             CHECKER B (PoS)   52
    PoS2   COMPOUND MEASURES
             CHECKER A (PoS/LD)   53
             CHECKER B (PoS/LD)   54

Ma4 Handling Data

LD1 Pupils specify hypotheses and test them by designing and using appropriate methods that take
     account of bias.
    PoS1   MAKING HYPOTHESES
             CHECKER A (PoS/LD)   55
             CHECKER B (PoS/LD)   56

LD2 They determine the modal class and estimate the mean, median and range of sets of grouped data,
     selecting the statistic most appropriate to their line of enquiry.
    PoS1   MODE, RANGE, MEAN AND MEDIAN FOR GROUPED DATA
             CHECKER A (PoS)   57
             CHECKER B (PoS)   58
    PoS2   USING GROUPED DATA
             CHECKER A (PoS/LD)   59
             CHECKER B (PoS/LD)   60

CONTENTS

Ma4, CONTINUED

LD3 They use measures of average and range, with associated frequency polygons, as appropriate, to compare distributions and make inferences.

PoS1 FREQUENCY POLYGONS

CHECKER A (PoS/LD)   61

CHECKER B (PoS/LD)   62

LD4 They draw a line of best fit on a scatter diagram, by inspection.

PoS1 LINES OF BEST FIT

CHECKER A (PoS/LD)   63

CHECKER B (PoS/LD)   64

LD5 Pupils understand relative frequency as an estimate of probability and use this to compare outcomes of experiments.

PoS1 RELATIVE FREQUENCY

CHECKER A (PoS/LD)   65

CHECKER B (PoS/LD)   66

Level by Level Mathematics National Curriculum CHECKERS			Level 7	
Name		Year	Class	

	Score or Grade		Notes	
Ma1 Tests				
LD1 PoS1 (PoS/LD) A ASKING QUESTIONS B				
LD2 PoS1 (PoS/LD) A MAKING IMPROVEMENTS B				
LD3 PoS1 (PoS/LD) A EXPLAINING SOLUTIONS B				
LD4 PoS1 (PoS/LD) A EXPLANATION AND EVIDENCE B				
Ma2 Tests				
LD1 PoS1 (PoS/LD) A MENTAL ESTIMATES B				
LD2 PoS1 (PoS/LD) A MULTIPLYING AND DIVIDING ... B				
LD3 PoS1 (PoS) A USING CALCULATOR MEMORY B				
LD3 PoS2 (PoS) A USING CALCULATOR BRACKETS B				
LD3 PoS3 (PoS/LD) A SOLVING PROBLEMS B				
LD4 PoS1 (PoS/LD) A PROPORTIONAL AMOUNTS B				
LD5 PoS1 (PoS) A RULES FOR SEQUENCES B				
LD5 PoS2 (PoS) A QUADRATIC RULES AND EXPRESSIONS B				
LD5 PoS3 (PoS/LD) A QUADRATIC RULES FOR SEQUENCES B				
LD6 PoS1 (PoS/LD) A SOLVING SIMULTANEOUS EQUATIONS USING GRAPHS B				
LD7 PoS1 (PoS/LD) A SOLVING SIMULTANEOUS EQUATIONS B				
LD8 PoS1 (PoS) A INEQUALITY STATEMENTS B				
LD8 PoS2 (PoS/LD) A SOLVING INEQUALITIES B				
Ma3 Tests				
LD1 PoS1 (PoS) A PYTHAGORAS' RULE B				
LD1 PoS2 (PoS/LD) A USING PYTHAGORAS' RULE B				
LD2 PoS1 (PoS) A CALCULATING LENGTHS AND AREAS B				

Name   Year   Class

	Score or Grade		Notes	

Ma3 continued

LD2 PoS2 (PoS) A VOLUMES OF PRISMS B				
LD2 PoS1-2 (LD) A LENGTH, AREA AND VOLUME B				
LD3 PoS1 (PoS/LD) A ENLARGING SHAPES B				
LD4 PoS1 (PoS/LD) A LOCUS B				
LD5 PoS1 (PoS/LD) A ACCURACY IN MEASUREMENTS B				
LD6 PoS1 (PoS) A DISTANCE, SPEED AND TIME B				
LD6 PoS2 (PoS/LD) A COMPOUND MEASURES B				

Ma4 Tests

LD1 PoS1 (PoS/LD) A MAKING HYPOTHESES B				
LD2 PoS1 (PoS) A MODE, RANGE, MEAN AND MEDIAN ... B				
LD2 PoS2 (PoS/LD) A USING GROUPED DATA B				
LD3 PoS1 (PoS/LD) A FREQUENCY POLYGONS B				
LD4 PoS1 (PoS/LD) A LINES OF BEST FIT B				
LD5 PoS1 (PoS/LD) A RELATIVE FREQUENCY B				
A B				
A B				
A B				
A B				
A B				
A B				
A B				
A B				

Ma1 █ LD1 █ PoS1 █ CHECKER A (PoS/LD)

LD1 █ Starting from problems or contexts that have been presented to them, pupils introduce questions
of their own, which generate fuller solutions.
PoS1 █ Asking questions.

A1 The 2 cm square has been divided
into 16 right angled triangles, all
with hypotenuse 1 cm long.

2 cm

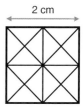

a) How many of the triangles
are there in a 3 cm square?

b) Ask yourself a more general
question about the number
of triangles in squares, and
answer it.

A2 The whole number mid-way between 9 and 17 is 13.
There is no whole number mid-way between 7 and 14.

a) Which whole number is mid-way between 30 and 42 ?

b) Write a more general question about mid-way numbers,
and answer it.

A3 The total length of straws needed
to make the 4 cm × 6 cm × 8 cm
cuboid frame is 72 cm.

4 cm   6 cm

8 cm

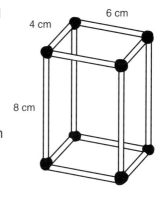

a) What is the total length of
straws needed to make a
2 cm × 5 cm × 10 cm cuboid
frame?

b) Write a more general question
about the length of straws
needed for cuboid frames,
and answer it.

A4 a) How many right angles can a
concave pentagon (5 sides) have?

b) Ask yourself how many right angles
a concave shape with a different
number of sides (ie not 5 sides)
can have, and answer it.

concave pentagons

A5 The diagram shows that the sum
of the first 4 odd numbers is 16.

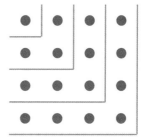

a) What is the sum of the first
10 odd numbers?

b) Ask yourself a more general
question about the sums of
sequences of odd numbers,
and answer it.

Ma1 LD1 PoS1 CHECKER B (PoS/LD)

LD1 — Starting from problems or contexts that have been presented to them, pupils introduce questions of their own, which generate fuller solutions.

PoS1 — Asking questions.

B1 Twelve small sticks are needed to make the 2 × 2 square of squares.

a) How many small sticks are needed to make a 3 × 3 square of squares?

b) Write a more general question about the number of sticks needed, and answer it.

B2 In the game you arrange the 7 cards for yourself into a line, throw the die, and move the counter.

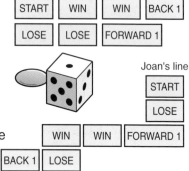

| START | WIN | WIN | BACK 1 |

| LOSE | LOSE | FORWARD 1 |

Joan's line

| START |
| LOSE |
| WIN | WIN | FORWARD 1 |
| BACK 1 | LOSE |

a) For Joan's line, what is the probability that she will win?

b) Write a question about probabilities for the game (but not about Joan's line), and answer it.

B3 In these chequerboard patterns the top left hand square is always black.

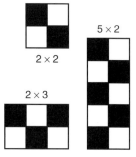

2 × 2

5 × 2

2 × 3

a) Is the number of black squares in a 3 × 6 board (3 rows and 6 columns), even or odd?

b) Write a question about the number of black squares for chequerboards with 5 columns, and answer it.

B4 These are *arms with hands* patterns. 9 sticks are needed to make A, and 25 sticks are needed to make B.

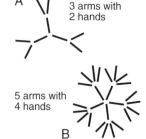

A — 3 arms with 2 hands

5 arms with 4 hands

B

a) How many sticks are needed to make a *6 arms with 3 hands* pattern?

b) Write a more general question about *arms with hands* patterns, and answer it.

B5 Look at the table. It gives the number of moons and stars in a set of patterns.

Number of moons	1	2	3	4	5	6
Number of stars	2	5	8	11	14	

a) What number is missing from the table?

b) Write a more general question about the patterns, and answer it.

LD2 　They examine critically and justify their choice of mathematical presentation, considering
　　　alternative approaches and explaining improvements they have made.
PoS1 　Making improvements.

A1 This is Sayeed's solution
to the fruit cage problem:

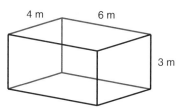

4 m   6 m   3 m

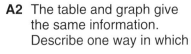

Amount needed =
$3 + 3 \times 2$
$+ 3 + 3 + 3 \times 2$
$+ 2 \times 6 = 42$ m.

a) Write Sayeed's solution
in a better way.

b) Describe one way in
which you think your
presentation is better.

This is a fruit cage.
How many metres of mesh are
needed to cover the sides and
the top?
The mesh can be bought in a
continuous roll, 2 m wide.

A2 The table and graph give
the same information.
Describe one way in which

a) the table is more useful
than the graph

b) the graph is more useful
than the table.

Hours of sunshine in Bradford, 2 - 8 July

M	T	W	T	F	S	S
1.2	2.3	4.3	2.5	4.6	4.8	2.2

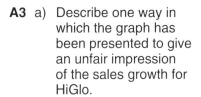

A3 a) Describe one way in
which the graph has
been presented to give
an unfair impression
of the sales growth for
HiGlo.

b) Make a sketch of a
graph which gives a
fairer impression of
sales growth.

HiGlo hair spray sales

A4 Carol is asked to compare numbers of saplings, young
trees and mature trees in Fairmile Wood.
She writes her results like this:

a) Write the results in a more useful way.

b) Give one reason why you think your
presentation is more useful.

Saplings	$\frac{17}{40}$
Young	$\frac{3}{8}$
Mature	$\frac{1}{5}$

A5 30 students took a written French test.
They went to Paris for 7 days, then took
the same test again.
The table shows the results.
The local newspaper wrote this headline:
ONE WEEK IN PARIS IMPROVES LEARNING

	Before Paris	After Paris
Mean	39.6	45.6
Range	14.0	14.8

a) Give one reason why the headline might be misleading.

b) Explain how the testing might be changed to give more
dependable results.

Ma1 ■ LD2 ■ PoS1 ■ CHECKER B (PoS/LD)

LD2 ■ They examine critically and justify their choice of mathematical presentation, considering alternative approaches and explaining improvements they have made.

PoS1 ■ Making improvements.

B1 The table and the scatter diagram give the same information. Give one way in which you think

a) the scatter diagram is more useful than the table

b) the table is more useful than the scatter diagram.

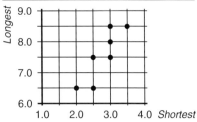

Lengths (in cm) of longest and shortest fingers for 7 people in a family

| Longest | 8.5 | 8.5 | 8.0 | 7.5 | 7.5 | 6.5 | 6.5 |
| Shortest | 3.0 | 3.5 | 3.0 | 2.5 | 3.0 | 2.0 | 2.5 |

B2 Wesley studies the number of visits made by female and male swallows to their nests to feed the young in one day. The table shows his results.

a) Present the results in a different, more useful way.

b) Give one reason why you think your presentation is more useful.

| female | 48 |
| male | 32 |

B3 The amount of rain in the summer of 1933 in Carlington was twice that in the summer of 1932.
The local newspaper printed the pictogram to compare the two years.

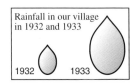

Rainfall in our village in 1932 and 1933

1932   1933

a) Describe one way in which the pictogram gives a misleading impression about the rainfall.

b) Draw what you think would be a fairer pictogram.

B4 Andrea is asked to calculate the area of the bow tie shape. This is her solution:

a) What does 96 represent?

b) Rewrite Andrea's solution so that it is easier to follow.

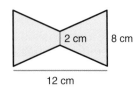

2 cm   8 cm

12 cm

96.
$\frac{1}{2} \times 12 \times 3 = 18.$
Area $= 96 - 18 - 18 = 60.$

B5 Pat measures the radius of a circle correct to 1 DP.
She writes:
Radius $= 4.0$ cm (1 DP).
Area estimate $= \pi r^2 = 50.272$ cm^2.

a) Why is her estimate for the area not sensible?

b) Write a more sensible estimate for the area, and show how you obtained it.

Ma1 LD3 PoS1 CHECKER A (PoS/LD)

LD3 Pupils justify their generalisations or solutions, showing some insight into the mathematical structure of the situation being investigated.

PoS1 Explaining solutions.

A1 Look at the sequence of dot patterns:

a) How many dots has the 50th pattern?

b) Explain your answer in part a).

A2 Look at the table of values.

a) Give another pair of values for x and y which fits the table.

b) The values of x and y are connected. Explain how a value of x can be found from the corresponding value of y.

x	y
0	2
1	4
4	10
6	14
9	20
15	32

A3 All of the numbers in a set are less than 500, and have 1, 2, 5 and 7 as factors.

a) 210 is one of the numbers. Find all the numbers in the set.

b) Why do all of the numbers have 0 as their units digit?

A4 a) Explain how to find the surface area of a cube when you know the edge length.

b) Explain how to find the edge length when you know the surface area.

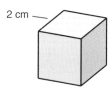

2 cm

The edge length of this cube is 2 cm

A5 ABCD is a rectangle drawn on a grid. The coordinates of A, B and C are:

A: $(a, 10)$, B: $(a + 3, 13)$, C: $(a + 5, 11)$.

a) Write down the x coordinate of D.

b) Explain your answer in part a).

Ma1 ▌LD3 ▌PoS1 ▌CHECKER B (PoS/LD)

LD3 ▌Pupils justify their generalisations or solutions, showing some insight into the mathematical structure of the situation being investigated.

PoS1 ▌Explaining solutions.

B1 These are the first three members of a sequence of dot patterns.

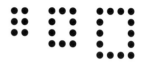

a) How many dots are there in the 50th pattern?

b) Explain your answer in part a).

B2 These are *Storeview* windows. All *Storeview* windows have the same proportions.

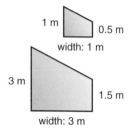

1 m   0.5 m
width: 1 m

3 m   1.5 m

width: 3 m

a) If the width of a window is $2h$ m, which of these is its area:

h^2 m², $2h^2$ m², $3h^2$ m² ?

b) Explain your answer in part a).

B3 A circle with a radius of 5 units is drawn on the grid, with its centre at (0, 0).

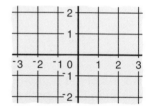

a) Is the point (3, 4) inside, on, or outside the circle?

b) Explain your answer in part a)

B4 The number chains are made by multiplying the previous number by 3 then subtracting 2.
Each chain starts with a whole number, and ends when a number larger than 100 is reached.

$2 - 4 - 10 - 28 - 82 - 244$

$7 - 19 - 55 - 163$

$5 - 13 - 37 - 109$

a) What is the smallest ending number that a chain can have?

b) Explain your answer in part a).

B5 Think about routes on the framework, which begin at A, P, Q or R and which arrive at or pass through all four vertices only once.

Examples:
A → P → Q → R
P → R → Q → A.

a) How many different routes are there?

b) Explain your answer in part a).

Ma1 ▪ LD4 ▪ PoS1 ▪ CHECKER A (PoS/LD)

LD4 ▪ They appreciate the difference between mathematical explanation and experimental evidence.
PoS1 ▪ Explanation and evidence.

A1 A bag contains 10 coloured beads.
Mike chooses a bead, records its colour, and replaces it.
He does this 10 times and gets a red bead 6 times and a white bead 4 times.

Write *true* or *false* for each of these:

a) The probability of choosing a red bead must be 0.6.

b) The probability of choosing a red bead must be greater than that of choosing a white bead.

A2 The nth number in a sequence is $4n + 1$.
The first number is 5.
Jo says that all the numbers must be odd.

a) Give two more examples of numbers from the sequence.

b) Explain why all the numbers in the sequence must be odd.

CITY OF PORTSMOUTH
BOYS' SCHOOL
LONDON ROAD, HILSEA
PORTSMOUTH PO2 9RJ
TEL 0705 693521
FAX 0705 665720

A3 Telina is finding all the decimal endings when a number is divided by 8.
She says that these are the possible endings:
.0, .125, .25, .5, .75, .875.

a) Give an example which she has missed.

b) Explain why we can get exactly 8 different decimal endings when we divide whole numbers by 8.

A4 The shapes are made by cutting a corner from the same size square.

a) Find the perimeter of each shape.
What do you notice?

b) Use a sketch of a shape like A, B and C to help you to explain what you discovered in part a).

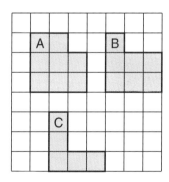

A5 Mark notices that 6 and 15 cannot be divided by 9, but their product, 6×15, can.
The same is true for 24×60.

a) Give another example.

b) Explain why the products of the numbers can be divided by 9.

Ma1 ▌LD4 ▌PoS1 ▌CHECKER B (PoS/LD)

LD4 ▮ They appreciate the difference between mathematical explanation and experimental evidence.
PoS1 ▮ Explanation and evidence.

B1 a) Liz spins the spinner 100 times.
She scores Red 40 times.
She says that the probability
of scoring Red must be 0.4.
Is she correct?

b) Calculate the probability of
scoring Blue.

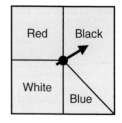

B2 a) Choose any number.
Multiply by 2 then add 2.
Start again with the same
number.
Add 1 then multiply by 2.
Try another starting number.
What do you notice?

b) Explain why the result you
observed in part a) is true
for any starting number.

B3 The squares are drawn on
a 1 cm square grid.

a) Explain why the number
of dots on the boundary
of all squares like these
is an even number.

b) What is special about
the number of dots
inside each square?

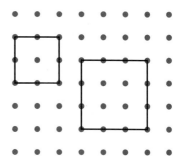

B4 Rajan says that some collections of 2 cm squares can be
arranged to make larger squares.

a) Use a drawing to show that he is correct for four 2 cm
squares.

b) Explain why two hundred and forty eight 2 cm squares
cannot be arranged to make a larger square.

B5 Explain why

a) the angle at the centre of a
regular polygon with 20 sides
is 18°

b) the angle at the centre of a
regular polygon cannot be16°.

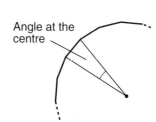

Angle at the
centre

Ma2 ▌LD1 ▌PoS1 ▌CHECKER A (PoS/LD)

LD1 ▌ In making estimates, pupils round to one significant figure and multiply and divide mentally.
PoS1 ▌ Mental estimates.

No Calculators

A1 The mass of the reel of cotton is 28 g.
42 reels are packed in a box.

a) Write a 1 SF approximation for
(i) the mass of the reel
(ii) the number of reels in the box.

b) Use your approximations in part a)
to estimate the total mass, in grams,
of a box of reels.

A2 a) Write a 1 SF approximation for
(i) 237   (ii) 18.

b) Use your approximations in
part a) to estimate the result
of 237 ÷ 18.

A3 a) On average, each pace Larry takes
is 0.53 m long.
Write this length correct to 1 SF.

b) It is 317 paces from Larry's house
to his Gran's house.

Use 1SF approximations to estimate
the distance, in metres, from Larry's
house to his Gran's house.

A4 a) Write a 1 SF approximation for
(i) 3.94   (ii) 0.012.

b) Use your approximations in
part a) to estimate the result
of 3.94 ÷ 0.012.

A5 a) 0.76 kg of cheese cost £1.90.
Estimate the cost of 1 kg.
Show how you make your estimate.

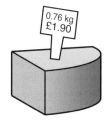

0.76 kg
£1.90

b) A bottle of medicine holds 0.215 *l*.
Estimate the total amount of medicine
in 86 bottles.
Show how you make your estimate.

Ma2 ▮ LD1 ▮ PoS1 ▮ CHECKER B (PoS/LD)

LD1 ▮ In making estimates, pupils round to one significant figure and multiply and divide mentally.
PoS1 ▮ Mental estimates.

No Calculators

B1 The ice lolly is made from 88 ml of water.
96 lollies are packed to a box.

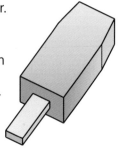

a) Write a 1 SF approximation for
   (i) the number of ml of water in each
     lolly
   (ii) the number of lollies in each box.

b) Use your approximations in part a)
to estimate the amount of water
used for a full box of lollies.

B2 a) Write a 1 SF approximation for
    (i) 17   (ii) 389.

b) Use your approximations in
part a) to estimate the result
of 389 ÷ 17.

B3 A machine prints 195 address labels
in 47.5 secs.

a) Write a 1 SF approximation for
    (i) 47.5   (ii) 195.

b) Use your approximations in part a)
to estimate the time taken to print
each label.

B4 a) Write a 1 SF approximation for
    (i) 0.0497   (ii) 0.909.

b) Use your approximations in
part a) to estimate the result
of 0.0497 × 0.909.

B5 A 5.1 m length of copper pipe has a mass
of 1.924 kg.

a) Estimate the mass of 1 m of the pipe.
Show how you make your estimate.

b) Estimate the mass of 20 m of the pipe.
Show how you make your estimate.

Ma2 LD2 PoS1 CHECKER A (PoS/LD)

LD2 — They understand the effects of multiplying and dividing by numbers between 0 and 1.
PoS1 — Multiplying and dividing by numbers less than 1.

No Calculators

A1 P is larger than Q.

   a) Which gives the larger result,
      $1.7 \times P$ or $1.7 \times Q$?

   b) Which gives the smaller result,
      $9.6 \div P$ or $9.6 \div Q$?

A2 Choose two of these numbers:
0.716, 0.94, 0.6.

Do not calculate.
Write down the division, $\square \div \square$,
which gives

   a) the largest result

   b) the smallest result.

A3 Choose two of these numbers:
0.349, 1.67, 0.69.

Do not calculate.
Write down the multiplication,
$\square \times \square$, which gives

   a) the largest result

   b) the smallest result.

A4 Think of the multiplication $0.226 \times N$.
Write down a value of N which gives
a result

   a) between 22.6 and 226

   b) between 0.00226 and 0.0226.

A5 Think of the division $7.49 \div T$.
Write down a value of T which
gives a result

   a) between 7.49 and 74.9

   b) between 0.749 and 7.49.

Ma2 LD2 PoS1 CHECKER B (PoS/LD)

LD2   They understand the effects of multiplying and dividing by numbers between 0 and 1.
PoS1   Multiplying and dividing by numbers less than 1.

No Calculators

B1   N is smaller than 1.
     K is larger than 1.

     a)   Which gives the larger result,
         $6.7 \div N$ or $6.7 \div K$?

     b)   Which gives the smaller result,
         $6.7 \times N$ or $6.7 \times K$?

B2   a) $17.9 \times T$ is less than 17.9.
         What can you say about T ?

     b) $17.9 \div R$ is smaller than 1.79.
         What can you say about R ?

B3   Choose two of these numbers:
     0.19,   7.68,   12.3.

     Do not calculate.
     Write down the division, $\square \div \square$,
     which gives

     a)   the largest result

     b)   the smallest result.

B4   Choose two of these numbers:
     8.79,   0.78,   0.0415.

     Do not calculate.
     Write down the multiplication,
     $\square \times \square$, which gives

     a)   the largest result

     b)   the smallest result.

B5   In part a) and part b),
     choose the best
     description from
     the list for Q.

     a) $1.01 \times Q = 0.746$

     b) $17.96 \div Q = 48.67$

A: Q is less than 0.1

B: Q lies between 0.1 and 1.0

C: Q lies between 1.0 and 10

D: Q lies between 10 and 100

Ma2 ▌LD3 ▌PoS1 ▌CHECKER A (PoS)

LD3 ▌ Pupils solve numerical problems involving multiplication and division with numbers of any size, using a calculator efficiently and appropriately.
PoS1 ▌ Using calculator memory.

A1 This key sequence puts 3.4 into calculator memory, then clears the display:

AC Min 3 . 4 M+ AC .

What do these put into calculator memory?

a) AC Min 5 + 9 M+ AC

b) AC Min 4 × 6 M+ AC

A2 a) Angus clears his calculator display and presses these keys:

MR × MR × MR + 5 = .

The display shows 32.
What number is in calculator memory?

b) Angus clears the display.
List the keys he should press now to add the content of the memory to 8.

A3 Calculate

a) $15.4 - 2.3^2$

b) $9 \div 2.4^2$.

A4 a) Put $6.2 \div 9.6$ into calculator memory.
Calculate $9.5 - 5.87$ and multiply the result by the content of the memory.
Write down the result correct to 2 DP.

b) Put 7.3×1.024 into calculator memory.
Calculate $3.7 \div 9.2$ and divide this by the content of the memory.
Write down the result correct to 2 DP.

A5 Put $\sqrt{3} \div 4$ into calculator memory.

a) Calculate one-seventh of the number in the memory.
Write the result correct to 2 DP.

b) Find the square root of the number in the memory.
Write the result correct to 2 DP.

Ma2 ▌LD3 ▌PoS1 ▌CHECKER B (PoS)

LD3 ▌ Pupils solve numerical problems involving multiplication and division with numbers of any size, using a calculator efficiently and appropriately.

PoS1 ▌ Using calculator memory.

B1 This key sequence puts 9.7 into calculator memory, then clears the display:

AC Min 9 • 7 M+ AC

What do these put into calculator memory?

a) AC Min 5 ÷ 2 M+ AC

b) AC Min 3 + 6 M+ AC

B2 a) Ritu presses these keys:

C MR + 1 • 2 = .

The result is 2.0.
What number is in calculator memory?

b) Linford presses these keys:

C 9 ÷ MR = .

The result is 0.09.
What number is in calculator memory?

B3 Divide 12 by 19, and put the result into calculator memory. Use the memory to help you to calculate, correct to 2 DP:

a) $4 - \frac{12}{19}$

b) $\frac{12}{19} + \frac{1}{7}$.

B4 Calculate:

a) $1.2^2 + 2.4^2$

b) $3.3^2 - 2.7^2$.

B5 Put 7.27×9.36 into calculator memory.

a) Divide 17.6 by the memory.
Write the result correct to 2 DP.

b) Multiply the memory by 15.87.
Write the result correct to 2 DP.

Ma2 ▮ LD3 ▮ PoS2 ▮ CHECKER A (PoS)

LD3   ▮ Pupils solve numerical problems involving multiplication and division with numbers of any size, using a calculator efficiently and appropriately.

PoS2   ▮ Using calculator brackets.

A1 Calculate:

    a) $(3.84 \div 3.2) \times 1.2$

    b) $3.84 \div (1.6 \times 0.6)$.

A2 Calculate, correct to 2 DP:

    a) $\dfrac{4.2}{3.7 + 9.5}$

    b) $\dfrac{4.2}{3.7} + \dfrac{1.5}{9.5}$.

A3 Sets of brackets are missing from the calculations in parts a) and b). Copy each calculation and write brackets in the correct positions.

    a) $2.1 \times 6.3 + 4.7 \times 8.9 = 205.59$

    b) $2.1 \times 6.3 + 4.7 \times 8.9 = 55.06$

CITY OF PORTSMOUTH
BOYS' SCHOOL
LONDON ROAD, HILSEA
PORTSMOUTH PO2 9RJ
TEL 0705 693521
FAX 0705 665720

A4 Calculate:

    a) $(12.6 - 3.9) \div (0.2 + 1.3)$

    b) $(12.6 + 3.9) \times (14.7 - 8.4)$.

A5 a) $A = \frac{1}{2}(a + b)h$.

       Find A when $a = 2.59$, $b = 6.79$ and $h = 8.32$.

    b) $P = \dfrac{2}{Q} + \dfrac{1}{N}$.

       Find P, correct to 2 DP, when $Q = 7$ and $N = 12$.

Ma2 ▮ LD3 ▮ PoS2 ▮ CHECKER B (PoS)

LD3   ▮ Pupils solve numerical problems involving multiplication and division with numbers of any size, using a calculator efficiently and appropriately.

PoS2 ▮ Using calculator brackets.

B1 Calculate:

    a) $7.5 \times (4.3 + 9.6)$

    b) $8.4 \times (9.3 - 4.5)$.

B2 Calculate, correct to 2 DP:

    a) $\dfrac{17}{19 - 3.7}$

    b) $\frac{1}{7} + \frac{1}{8}$.

B3 Sets of brackets are missing from the calculations in parts a) and b). Copy each calculation and write brackets in the correct positions.

    a) $6.4 \div 3.6 \div 2.4 \ = \ 4.27$ (2 DP)

    b) $3.2 \div 1.8 \div 1.2 \ = \ 1.48$ (2 DP)

B4 Calculate:

    a) $3 \times (4.8 + 9.6) + 4 \times (4.3 - 2.7)$

    b) $(17.7 - 14.9) \times (4.3 + 4.8)$.

B5 a) $R \ = \ \dfrac{C}{T - K}$

        Find R, correct to 3 SF, when
        $C = 10$, $T = 7$ and $K = 4.6$.

     b) $N \ = \ \frac{1}{2}b + k^2$

        Find N, correct to 3 SF, when
        $b = 4.6$ and $k = 7.2$.

Ma2 LD3 PoS3 CHECKER A (PoS/LD)

LD3   Pupils solve numerical problems involving multiplication and division with numbers of any size, using a calculator efficiently and appropriately.

PoS3   Solving problems.

Use your calculator, but show clearly how you solve each problem.

A1 a) 0.72 kg of cheese cost £1.71.
Find the cost of 1 kg, correct to the nearest 1p.

b) The mass of 600 identical buttons is 7.2 kg.
Calculate the mass, in grams, of each button.

A2 a) Calculate the area of shape A.

b) Shape B is a square with a square hole. Calculate its area.

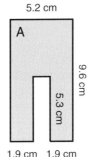

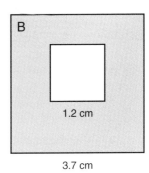

A3 a) The volume of water in the glass is $\pi \times 4.1^2 \times 6$ ml.
Mike drinks one-quarter of the water.
How many ml of water are left?
Write your result correct to the nearest ml.

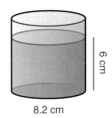

b) The volume of orange in the glass is $\frac{1}{3} \times \pi \times 3^2 \times 4.8$ ml.
Liz drinks a half of the orange.
How many ml are left?
Write your result correct to the nearest ml.

A4 a) It is 13.75 km from Marling bus station to Parkford bus station, and 18.6 km from Parkford bus station to Bannerton bus station.
In 36 bus journeys from Marling to Bannerton and back, how many km do I travel?

b) 34 750 bricks are dried in a kiln.
Before drying, each brick has a mass of 4.6 kg.
Each brick loses 23 % of its mass during drying.
What is the total mass of the dried bricks, correct to the nearest tonne?

A5 a) Write down a multiplication, $\square \times \square$, involving two numbers less than 1 which gives the result 0.9408.

b) Write down a division, $\square \div \square$, involving two numbers less than 0.5 which gives the result 6.5.

Ma2 ▌LD3 ▌PoS3 ▌CHECKER B (PoS/LD)

LD3 ▌ Pupils solve numerical problems involving multiplication and division with numbers of any size,
using a calculator efficiently and appropriately.
PoS3 ▌ Solving problems.

Use your calculator, but show clearly how you solve each problem.

B1 1 kg of elderberries gives 0.35 *l* of juice.

   a) How many litres of juice should you get from 2.6 kg ?

   b) How many kg of elderberries are needed for 1 *l* of juice?
Write the result correct to 1 DP.

B2 a) 10 000 cm² = 1 m².
A kitchen floor is covered exactly by 317 rectangular tiles, each measuring 24 cm × 30 cm.
What is the area of the floor, correct to the nearest 0.1 m² ?

   b) The mass of the contents of a tin of toffees is 0.24 kg.
The mass of the tin is 0.032 kg.
What is the total mass, in kg, of 350 tins of toffees?

B3 a) The height of the cone

is $\dfrac{3 \times 198}{\pi \times 5.32^2}$ cm.

Calculate the height correct to 1 DP.

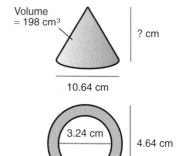

Volume = 198 cm³
? cm
10.64 cm

   b) The area of the face of the washer is $\pi(2.32^2 - 1.62^2)$ cm².

Calculate this correct to 1 DP.

3.24 cm
4.64 cm

B4 a) The formula for the circumference, C, of a circle of diameter D is $C = \pi D$.
Each of the four arms of the windmill is 7.35 m long.
How far, to the nearest metre, does the tip of an arm (eg, point P) travel in 50 turns?

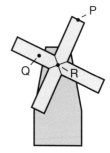

P
Q
R

   b) In one full turn point Q travels 20 m.
Find the distance QR correct to 1 DP.

B5 a) Don squares 7.68 then subtracts the square root of 7.68.
Write down his result correct to 2 DP.

   b) Carla divides 18.04 by 7.6 then divides 4.8 by the result.
Write down her result correct to 2 DP.

Ma2 LD4 PoS1 CHECKER A (PoS/LD)

LD4 They understand and use proportional changes.
PoS1 Proportional amounts.

A1 3 cup cakes cost £1.04.

a) How much do 9 cost?

b) How many can you buy for £10.40 ?

A2 The mass of a 5.2 m wooden plank is 6.8 kg.

a) A piece of the plank is 1.3 m long. What is its mass?

b) A piece of the plank has a mass of 2.3 kg. How long is it, correct to the nearest cm?

A3 Would you expect these to increase in direct proportion to each other? Write 'yes' or 'no' for each. If you write 'no', explain why.

a) The number of apples put into a barrel and the total mass of the apples.

b) The number of cars crossing a bridge, and the total number of passengers in the cars.

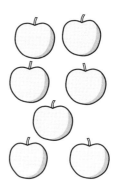

A4 X and Y vary in direct proportion to each other. X is 4 when Y is 7.

a) What is Y when X is 12 ?

b) What is X when Y is 35 ?

A5 a) Which graph, A, B or C, shows x and y varying in direct proportion to each other?

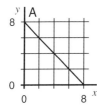 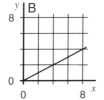 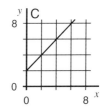

b) Copy and complete the table so that P and Q vary in direct proportion to each other.

P	?	6	9	21
Q	3	9	?	?

Ma2 LD4 PoS1 CHECKER B (PoS/LD)

LD4   They understand and use proportional changes.
PoS1   Proportional amounts.

B1 200 identical sheets of paper have
a total mass of 3 kg.

  a) What is the mass of 50 sheets?

  b) What is the mass of 750 sheets?

B2 1.2 kg of potatoes cost £1.62.

  a) Find the cost of 2 kg.

  b) What mass of potatoes
    can I buy for £3.78 ?

B3 Would you expect these to increase
in direct proportion to each other?
Write 'yes' or 'no' for each.
If you write 'no', explain why.

  a) The number of letters I post
    and the total cost.

  b) The total mass of a tin of toffees
    and the number of toffees in it,
    as I eat the toffees, one by one.

B4 L and M vary in direct proportion
to each other.
L is 9 when M is 24.

  a) What is M when L is 6 ?

  b) What is L when M is 6 ?

B5 a) Look at the graph.
    x and y vary in
    direct proportion
    to each other.
    The point (6, 8)
    shows one pair of
    values for x and y.
    Write down another
    pair of values.

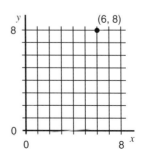

  b) Copy and complete the table
    so that A and B vary in direct
    proportion to each other.

A	?	8	14	?
B	7	14	?	98

A1 Find the 20th term of each sequence.

a) 1, 5, 9, 13, 17, …

b) 98, 97, 96, 95, 94, …

A2 Write down the *n*th term of each sequence.

a) 3, 4, 5, 6, 7, …

b) 4, 6, 8, 10, 12, …

A3 a) The *n*th term of a sequence is $3n + 2$.
Write down the 50th term.

b) The *n*th term of a sequence is $200 - 3n$.
Write down the 50th term.

A4 Look at the list.
Decide which one of A - D is the *n*th term of the sequence:

a) ⁻1, 1, 3, 5, 7, …

b) 5, 8, 11, 14, 17, …

A	$3n - 2$
B	$2n - 3$
C	$3n + 2$
D	$2n + 3$

A5 Find the *n*th term of each sequence.

a) 4, 10, 16, 22, 28, …

b) ⁻2, 2, 6, 10, 14, …

Ma2 ▌LD5 ▌PoS1 ▌CHECKER B (PoS)

LD5   ▌Pupils find and describe in symbols the next term or nth term of a sequence where the rule is quadratic.
PoS1   ▌Rules for sequences.

B1 Find the 20th term of each sequence.

    a) 2, 4, 6, 8, 10, ...

    b) 5, 7, 9, 11, 13, ...

B2 Write down the nth term of each sequence.

    a) 5, 6, 7, 8, 9, ...

    b) 100, 99, 98, 97, 96, ...

B3 a) The nth term of a sequence is $2n + 3$.
       Write down the 100th term.

    b) The nth term of a sequence is $200 - 2n$.
       Write down the 50th term.

B4 Look at the list.
Decide which one of A - D is the nth term of the sequence:

    a) 7, 11, 15, 19, 23, ...

    b) ⁻1, 2, 5, 8, 11, ...

A	$3n - 4$
B	$3n + 4$
C	$4n - 3$
D	$4n + 3$

B5 Find the nth term of each sequence.

    a) 9, 19, 29, 39, 49, ...

    b) 16, 21, 26, 31, 36, ...

Ma2 LD5 PoS2 CHECKER A (PoS)

LD5   Pupils find and describe in symbols the next term or nth term of a sequence where the rule is quadratic.

PoS2   Quadratic rules and expressions

A1 Find the value of each expression when $t = 4$.

a) $(t + 1)^2$

b) $25 - t^2$

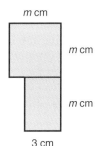

A2 a) Look at the diagram. Write down an expression for the total area of the figure.

b) In a shop there are k boxes of chocolates with $2k$ chocolates in each box. How many chocolates is this?

A3 a) t is a positive whole number. Find the smallest value of t for which t^2 is larger than $10t$.

b) Rajan says that $p^2 - 10$ is always larger than $10 - p^2$. Explain why he is wrong.

CITY OF PORTSMOUTH
BOYS' SCHOOL
LONDON ROAD, HILSEA
PORTSMOUTH PO2 9RJ
TEL 0705 693521
FAX 0705 665720

A4 Find the value of $n^2 + n - 1$

a) when $n = 3$

b) when $n = 0.5$.

A5 Look at the table. Write down the number that is represented by

a) A

b) B.

n	$60 - n^2$
1	59
2	A
B	11

Ma2 ▮ LD5 ▮ PoS2 ▮ CHECKER B (PoS)

LD5 ▮ Pupils find and describe in symbols the next term or nth term of a sequence where the rule is quadratic.

PoS2 ▮ Quadratic rules and expressions

B1 Find the value of each expression when $p = 3$.

a) $(p + 2)^2$

b) $39 - p^2$

B2 Look at the list. Choose the expression for the surface area of

a) the cube

b) the cuboid.

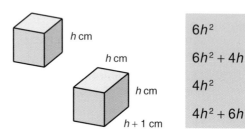

$6h^2$

$6h^2 + 4h$

$4h^2$

$4h^2 + 6h$

B3 a) t is a positive whole number. Find the largest value of t for which $(t - 1)^2$ is smaller than 110.

b) George says that $2e^2$ is always larger than $2e$. Explain why he is wrong.

B4 Find the value of $4n^2 + n - 7$

a) when $n = 0$

b) when $n = 2$.

B5 Look at the table. Write down the number that is represented by

a) A

b) B.

n	$5 - 2n^2$
1	3
2	A
B	⁻45

Ma2 ▮ LD5 ▮ PoS3 ▮ CHECKER A (PoS/LD)

LD5 ▮ Pupils find and describe in symbols the next term or *n*th term of a sequence where the rule is quadratic.

PoS3 ▮ Quadratic rules for sequences.

A1 Write down the next term of each sequence.

   a) 2, 5, 10, 17, 26, 37, ...

   b) 0, 3, 8, 15, 24, 35, ...

A2 Write down the 10th term of each sequence.

   a) 1, 4, 9, 16, 25, 36, ...

   b) 3, 6, 11, 18, 27, 38, ...

A3 a) The *n*th term of a sequence is $n^2 + 4$.
      Write down the first 3 terms.

   b) The *n*th term of a sequence is $5 - n^2$.
      Write down the first 3 terms.

A4 Find the 8th term of each sequence.

   a) $S_n = 3n^2$

   b) $S_n = 2n^2 - 9$

A5 Find the *n*th term of each sequence.

   a) 2, 8, 18, 32, 50, ...

   b) 6, 15, 30, 51, 78, ...

Ma2 LD5 PoS3 CHECKER B (PoS/LD)

LD5 ▪ Pupils find and describe in symbols the next term or nth term of a sequence where the rule is quadratic.

PoS3 ▪ Quadratic rules for sequences.

B1 Write down the next term of each sequence.

    a) 3, 6, 11, 18, 27, 38, ...

    b) 5, 8, 13, 20, 29, 40, ...

B2 Write down the 10th term of each sequence.

    a) 2, 5, 10, 17, 26, 37, ...

    b) 7, 10, 15, 22, 31, 42, ...

B3 a) The nth term of a sequence is $n^2 + 6$.
      Write down the first 3 terms.

    b) The nth term of a sequence is $8 - n^2$.
      Write down the first 3 terms.

B4 Find the 12th term of each sequence.

    a) $S_n = 2n^2$

    b) $S_n = 3n^2 - 5$

B5 Find the nth term of each sequence.

    a) ⁻3, 0, 5, 12, 21, ...

    b) 7, 16, 31, 52, 79, ...

Ma2 LD6 PoS1 CHECKER A (PoS/LD)

LD6 Pupils use graphical methods to solve simultaneous linear equations in two variables.
PoS1 Solving simultaneous equations: using graphs.

You need squared paper for Q5.

A1 Use Graph A.

Find the solution to the simultaneous equations

a) $x + y = 6$
   and
   $y = 2x$

b) $x + y = 6$
   and
   $x = 2y$.

Graph A

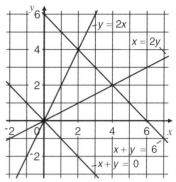

A2 Use Graph A

a) to find the solution to the simultaneous equations $y = 2x$ and $x = 2y$

b) to help you to explain why the simultaneous equations $x + y = 6$ and $x + y = 0$ have no solution.

Graph B

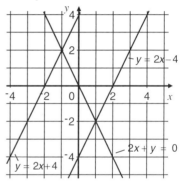

A3 Use Graph B.

Find the solution to the simultaneous equations

a) $y = 2x + 4$
   and
   $2x + y = 0$

b) $y = 2x - 4$
   and
   $2x + y = 0$.

Graph C

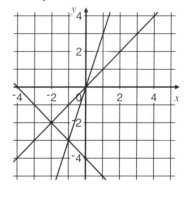

A4 Use Graph C.

Find the solution to the simultaneous equations

a) $y = 3x$
   and
   $x + y + 4 = 0$

b) $y = x$
   and
   $x + y + 4 = 0$.

A5 *Use squared paper.*
Sketch graphs to help you to find the solution to the simultaneous equations

a) $y = x + 1$ and $x + y = 0$

b) $y = 4x$ and $x + y + 5 = 0$.

Ma2 LD6 PoS1 CHECKER B (PoS/LD)

LD6 ▪ Pupils use graphical methods to solve simultaneous linear equations in two variables.
PoS1 ▪ Solving simultaneous equations: using graphs.

You need squared paper for Q5.

B1 Use Graph A.

Find the solution to the simultaneous equations

a) $x + y = 4$
and
$x = 3y$

b) $2x + y = 4$
and
$y = 2x$.

Graph A

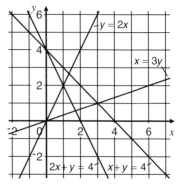

B2 Use Graph A

a) to find the solution to the simultaneous equations
$y = 2x$ and $x = 3y$

b) to help you to explain why the x and y values which satisfy both
$x + y = 4$ and $y = 2x$
are not whole numbers.

Graph B

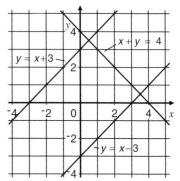

B3 Use Graph B.

Find the solution to the simultaneous equations

a) $y = x + 3$
and
$x + y = 4$

b) $y = x - 3$
and
$x + y = 4$.

Graph C

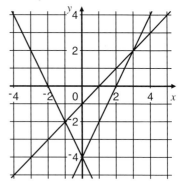

B4 Use Graph C.

Find the solution to the simultaneous equations

a) $y = x - 1$
and
$y = 2x - 4$

b) $y + 2x + 4 = 0$
and
$y = x - 1$.

B5 *Use squared paper.*
Sketch graphs to help you to find the solution to the simultaneous equations

a) $y = 2 - x$ and $y = x - 4$

b) $y + x = 8$ and $2y = x - 2$.

Ma2 ■ LD7 ■ PoS1 ■ CHECKER A (PoS/LD)

LD7 ■ Pupils use algebraic methods to solve simultaneous linear equations in two variables.
PoS1 ■ Solving simultaneous equations.

A1 Solve the simultaneous equations.

    a) $x + y = 2$
       and
       $y - x = 2$

    b) $p - 2q = 4$
       and
       $p + 2q = 6$

A2 Solve the simultaneous equations.

    a) $m + n = 4$
       and
       $3m + n = 6$

    b) $2k + 3t = 8$
       and
       $2k + t = 4$

A3 Solve the simultaneous equations.

    a) $m + 2n = 11$
       and
       $2m + n = 10$

    b) $k - 3t = 1$
       and
       $t + 2k = 9$

A4 Solve the simultaneous equations.

    a) $2m = n$
       and
       $8m - n = 12$

    b) $3p - q = 0$
       and
       $p + 2q = 14$

A5 Solve the simultaneous equations.

    a) $3k - 2h = 8$
       and
       $2k + 3h = 14$

    b) $5n - 2m = 9$
       and
       $3n - 5m = 13$

Ma2 ▪ LD7 ▪ PoS1 ▪ CHECKER B (PoS/LD)

LD7 ▪ Pupils use algebraic methods to solve simultaneous linear equations in two variables.
PoS1 ▪ Solving simultaneous equations.

B1 Solve the simultaneous equations.

a) $p + q = 4$
and
$p - q = 4$

b) $n - 2m = 3$
and
$2m + n = 7$

B2 Solve the simultaneous equations.

a) $b + 3c = 2$
and
$b + c = 0$

b) $5m + 2p = 12$
and
$2m + 2p = 6$

B3 Solve the simultaneous equations.

a) $t = 5n$
and
$4n + 2t = 28$

b) $d - c = 0$
and
$2c = d + 2$

B4 Solve the simultaneous equations.

a) $3t + k = 7$
and
$2t + 3k = 7$

b) $2n - 5m = 1$
and
$3n - 10m = 4$

B5 Solve the simultaneous equations.

a) $3p - 4n = 7$
and
$2p - 3n = 4$

b) $4x + 3y = 2$
and
$3x + 4y = 5$

Ma2 LD8 PoS1 CHECKER A (PoS)

LD8   They solve simple inequalities.
PoS1   Inequality statements.

A1 Match each inequality with one of the statements A, B, C, D.

    A p is greater than 2

    B p is greater than or equal to 2

    C p is less than 2

    D p is less than or equal to 2

  a) $p > 2$

  b) $p \leq 2$

A2 These are examples of inequality sentences:
$t \geq 4$; $3 \leq e < 8$.
Write an inequality sentence to represent each of these statements.

  a) The radius (r cm) of a circle is greater than 3 cm but less than 4 cm.

  b) The diameter (d cm) of a circle is less than or equal to 12 cm but larger than 6 cm.

A3 Write down which of the inequality statements P, Q, R, and S represents the set of numbers

    P $^{-}1 \leq g < 2$, g an integer

    Q $^{-}2 < g < 1$, g an integer

    R $^{-}2 \leq g < 1$, g an integer

    S $^{-}2 \leq g \leq 1$, g an integer

  a) $^{-}1$, 0, 1

  b) $^{-}2$, $^{-}1$, 0, 1.

A4 Look at the diagrams P and Q.
● means that the number is included in the set.
O means that the number is not included in the set.

Write an inequality sentence to represent the set of numbers shown in

  a) diagram P

  b) diagram Q.

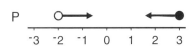

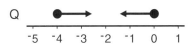

A5 a) $p > 5$.
    Copy and complete:
    $2p + 3 > \ldots\ldots$

  b) $k \leq 3$.
    Copy and complete:
    $7 - k \ldots 4$.

Ma2 ▮ LD8 ▮ PoS1 ▮ CHECKER B (PoS)

LD8 ▮ They solve simple inequalities.
PoS1 ▮ Inequality statements.

B1 Match each inequality with one of the statements A, B, C, D.

a) $k \leq 4$

b) $k > 4$

A k is greater than 4

B k is greater than or equal to 4

C k is less than 4

D k is less than or equal to 4

B2 a) George has more than £36 in his savings account.
He writes $m > 36$.
He withdraws £20.
Write a new inequality sentence which gives the new values of m.

b) Ritu has less than 300 g of jam left in her jam jar.
She writes $j < 300$.
She buys another 500 g.
Write a new inequality sentence for the new values of j.

B3 Write down which of the inequality statements P, Q, R, and S represents the set of numbers

a) ⁻3, ⁻2, ⁻1, 0, 1

b) ⁻2, ⁻1, 0, 1, 2.

P $^{-}3 \leq k < 2$, k an integer

Q $^{-}3 < k < 1$, k an integer

R $^{-}2 \leq k < 3$, k an integer

S $^{-}2 \leq k \leq 3$, k an integer

B4 Look at the number line diagram.
● means that the number is included in the set.
○ means that the number is not included in the set.

a) Write an inequality sentence to represent the set of numbers shown by the diagram.

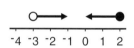

b) Draw a number line diagram to represent the set of numbers $^{-}4 \leq h < 3$.

B5 a) $y \geq 6$.
Two of A, B, C and D are true.
Which two?

b) $n < 7$.
Copy and complete:
$3n + 8 < \ldots\ldots$

A $y + 3 \leq 15$

B $y + 3 \geq 9$

C $9 - y \geq 3$

D $9 - y \leq 3$

Ma2 LD8 PoS2 CHECKER A (PoS/LD)

LD8   They solve simple inequalities.
PoS2   Solving inequalities.

A1 Solve each inequality.

  a) $k + 4 \leq 9$

  b) $k - 3 > 4$

A2 Solve each inequality.

  a) $2p \leq 18$

  b) $p \div 3 > 5$

A3 Solve each inequality.

  a) $2n + 1 \geq 11$

  b) $4 + 3n < 7$

A4 Solve each inequality.

  a) $3(n + 1) \leq 15$

  b) $4(n - 1) < 24$

A5 Solve each inequality.

  a) $5p + 1 > 2p + 10$

  b) $34 - 3p \leq 25$

Ma2 LD8 PoS2 CHECKER B (PoS/LD)

LD8 ▮ They solve simple inequalities.
PoS2 ▮ Solving inequalities.

B1 Solve each inequality.

    a) $d + 2 \leq 12$

    b) $d - 1 < 4$

B2 Solve each inequality.

    a) $3k \geq 9$

    b) $k \div 5 > 6$

B3 Solve each inequality.

    a) $2n + 1 > 9$

    b) $3 + 5n \leq 23$

B4 Solve each inequality.

    a) $2(m + 1) \leq 12$

    b) $3(m - 4) > 6$

B5 Solve each inequality.

    a) $4p + 3 > p + 21$

    b) $9 - 2p < 3$

Ma3 ▌LD1 ▌PoS1 ▌CHECKER A (PoS)

LD1 ▌ Pupils understand and apply Pythagoras' theorem when solving problems in two dimensions.
PoS1 ▌ Pythagoras' Rule.

A1 The diagrams show three squares drawn on the sides of right-angled triangles.

Calculate the area of

a) square Q

b) square R.

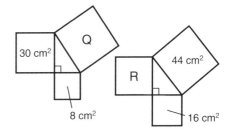

A2 The diagrams show triangles with squares drawn on their sides.

Explain how we can tell that

a) triangle J does not have a right angle.

b) triangle K does have a right angle.

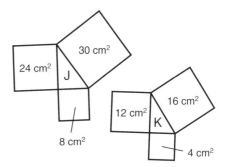

A3 The diagram shows a right-angled triangle with squares drawn on its sides.

Calculate, correct to 1 DP,

a) the length of TS

b) the length of RS.

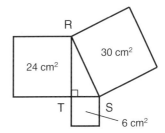

A4 The diagram shows a right-angled triangle with squares drawn on two of its sides.

Calculate

a) the length of EF, correct to 1 DP

b) the length of DF.

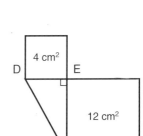

A5 a) In triangle RST, calculate the length of RS, correct to 1 DP.

b) In triangle LMN, calculate the length of MN, correct to 1 DP.

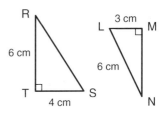

Ma3 LD1 PoS1 CHECKER B (PoS)

LD1 ▮ Pupils understand and apply Pythagoras' theorem when solving problems in two dimensions.
PoS1 ▮ Pythagoras' Rule.

B1 The diagrams show
three squares drawn
on the sides of
right-angled triangles.

Calculate the area of

a) square L

b) square M.

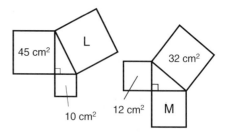

B2 a) Does triangle RST have a
right angle?
Explain your answer.

b) Three squares have areas
7 cm², 5 cm² and 12 cm².
Make a sketch to show how
the squares fit the sides of
a right-angled triangle.
Show clearly which angle in
the triangle is a right angle.

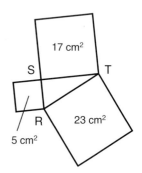

B3 The diagram shows a
right-angled triangle
with squares drawn on
its sides.

Calculate, correct to 1 DP,

a) the length of PQ

b) the length of PR.

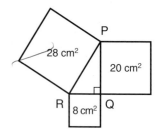

B4 The diagram shows a
right-angled triangle
with squares drawn on
two if its sides.

Calculate, correct to 1 DP,

a) the length of AB

b) the length of BC.

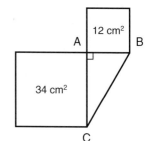

B5 a) In triangle PQR, calculate
the length of PQ, correct
to 1 DP.

b) In triangle LMN, calculate
the length of MN, correct
to 1 DP.

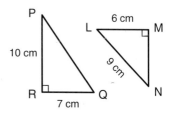

Ma3 LD1 PoS2 CHECKER A (PoS/LD)

LD1   Pupils understand and apply Pythagoras' theorem when solving problems in two dimensions.
PoS2   Using Pythagoras' Rule.

A1 a) An isosceles right-angled triangle has two
          sides 6 cm long.
          Calculate the length of the hypotenuse,
          correct to 1 DP.

   b) Calculate, correct to 1 DP, the lengths of the
       two shorter sides of a right-angled isosceles
       triangle with hypotonuse 6 cm long.

A2 a) Calculate the height,
          h cm, of the isosceles
          triangle ABC.

   b) Calculate the height of
       an equilateral triangle
       with sides 10 cm, correct
       to the nearest 0.1 cm.

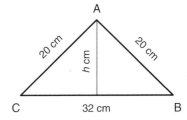

A3 The grid is drawn on 1 cm squared
    paper.

   a) How far apart are points A(0, 0)
       and B(3, 4) ?

   b) The circle has radius 2 cm.
       Use Pythagoras' Rule to decide
       whether the point P(1.8, 0.8) is
       inside or outside of the circle.
       Show how you decide.

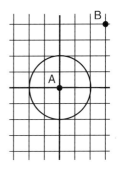

A4 The diagram shows
    the side view of a barn.
    The angle at A is 90°.
    Calculate, correct to
    the nearest 0.1 m,

   a) the width, w metres,
       of the building

   b) the height, h metres,
       of the building.

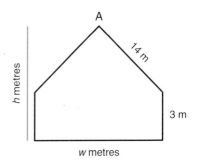

A5 Look at the
    diagram.
    calculate,
    correct to
    1 DP, the
    length of

   a) LO

   b) LP.

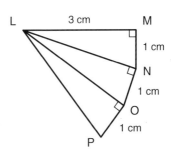

Ma3 LD1 PoS2 CHECKER B (PoS/LD)

LD1 ▪ Pupils understand and apply Pythagoras' theorem when solving problems in two dimensions.
PoS2 ▪ Using Pythagoras' Rule.

B1 a) Calculate the length of the
diagonals of a 16 cm × 12 cm
rectangle.

  b) Calculate the length of the
diagonals of a 5 cm square
correct to the nearest 0.1 cm.

B2 a) The area of a square field is 6241 m².
Calculate the diagonal distance across
the field correct to the nearest metre.

  b) A square field has a diagonal length
of 60 m.
Calculate the length of side of the field,
correct to the nearest metre.

B3 The step ladder has two sides
3 m long.

  a) Calculate the distance of A
above the ground, correct to
the nearest 10 cm, when BC
is 2 m.

  b) Calculate the distance apart
of B and C, correct to the
nearest 10 cm, when A is
2.9 m above the ground.

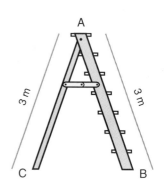

B4 Shape ABCD is
a right-angled
trapezium.

  a) Calculate BC.

  b) Calculate AC,
correct to 1 DP.

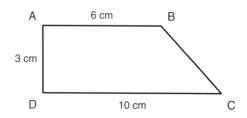

B5 PQRS is a
section of
a roof space.

Calculate,
correct to
1 DP,

  a) QS

  b) PS.

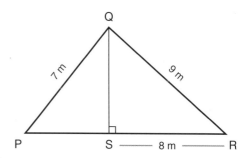

Ma3 ▌LD2 ▌PoS1 ▌CHECKER A (PoS)
LD2 ▌They calculate lengths, areas and volumes in plane shapes and right prisms.
PoS1 ▌Calculating lengths and areas.

Useful formulae

Area of a circle $= \pi \times$ radius^2
Perimeter of a circle $= \pi \times$ diameter
Area of a triangle $= \frac{1}{2} \times$ base length $\times$ height

A1 The shape is made by cutting
a rectangle from a square card.

a) How much longer is the
perimeter of the square
than the rectangle?

b) Calculate the area of the
grey section.

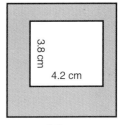

A2 The shape is made from a
6 cm square and an isosceles
right-angled triangle.

a) Calculate h.

b) Calculate BC, correct to
the nearest 0.1 cm.

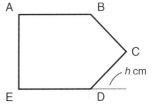

A3 The area of rhombus
ABCD is 42 cm^2.
DB = 12 cm.

Calculate

a) the area of ABX

b) the distance AC.

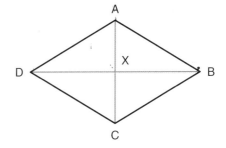

A4 The shape is made from an 8 cm
square and two semi-circles.
Calculate

a) the perimeter of the shape,
correct to the nearest 0.1 cm

b) the area of the shape, correct
to the nearest 0.1 cm^2.

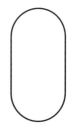

A5 The cuboid measures
10 cm $\times$ 14 cm $\times$ 9 cm.

Calculate, correct to
the nearest 0.1 cm,

a) IG

b) EG.

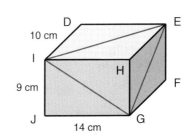

Ma3 ▮ LD2 ▮ PoS1 ▮ CHECKER B (PoS)

LD2 ▮ They calculate lengths, areas and volumes in plane shapes and right prisms.
PoS1 ▮ Calculating lengths and areas.

Useful formulae

Area of a circle $= \pi \times \text{radius}^2$
Perimeter of a circle $= \pi \times \text{diameter}$
Area of a triangle $= \frac{1}{2} \times \text{base length} \times \text{height}$

B1 Triangle ABC is made from two right-angled triangles.
AX = 10 cm; CB = 12 cm.

The area of triangle ABX is half the area of triangle CXA.

Calculate

a) the area of triangle CAB

b) the length of CX.

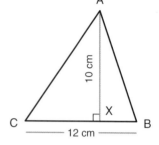

B2 The shape is made from an equilateral triangle with sides 8 cm long, and a semi-circle.

Calculate

a) the area of the semi-circle, correct to the nearest 0.1 cm^2

b) the height, h cm, of the shape, correct to the nearest 0.1 cm.

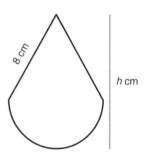

B3 ABC is an isosceles triangle with base length 13 cm.

a) Calculate the height, h cm, of the triangle, correct to the nearest 0.1 cm.

b) Calculate the area of the triangle, correct to the nearest 0.1 cm^2.

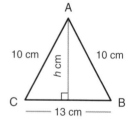

B4 Shape PQRS is a right-angled trapezium with area 140 cm^2.
PQ = 17 cm; RS = 11 cm.

a) Calculate PS.

b) Calculate the area of triangle QRS correct to the nearest 0.1 cm^2.

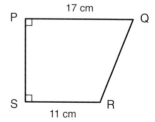

B5 The area of a rhombus is 400 cm^2.
The length of the longer diagonal is 40 cm.

a) Calculate the length of the shorter diagonal.

b) Calculate the lengths of the sides, correct to the nearest 0.1 cm.

Ma3 LD2 PoS2 CHECKER A (PoS)

LD2 They calculate lengths, areas and volumes in plane shapes and right prisms.
PoS2 Volumes of prisms.

Useful formulae

Volume of a prism = base area × height
Volume of a cylinder = π × radius² × height

A1 a) The volume of prism A
is 40 cm³.
What is the area of the
grey face?

b) The volume of prism B
is 54 cm³.
The area of the grey
face is 6 cm².
Calculate the length.

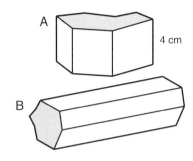

A2 Look at the two
prisms.

a) Calculate
the volume
of prism A.

c) Calculate
the volume
of prism B.

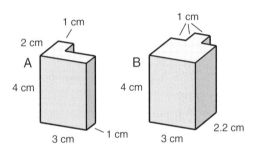

A3 a) The area of the base of a baked bean tin is 87 cm².
The height of the tin is 15 cm.
Calculate the volume.

b) A wooden rod has a volume of 18 cm³.
The area of its cross section is 4 cm².
How long is the rod?

A4 a) Calculate the volume
of the wedge.

b) Another wedge is 2 cm
longer than that in the
diagram.
How many cubic cm
greater is the volume?

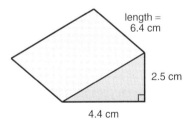

length =
6.4 cm

2.5 cm

4.4 cm

A5 a) Calculate the volume
of the cylinder, correct
to the nearest 1 cm³.

b) A £1 coin is 3 mm thick
and has a diameter of
23.5 mm.
Calculate the volume of
metal used to make it,
correct to the nearest
1 mm³.

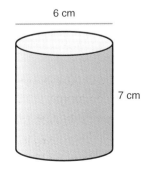

6 cm

7 cm

Ma3 LD2 PoS2 CHECKER B (PoS)

LD2   They calculate lengths, areas and volumes in plane shapes and right prisms.
PoS2   Volumes of prisms.

Useful formulae

Volume of a prism = base area × height
Volume of a cylinder = π × radius² × height

B1 Look at the two prisms.

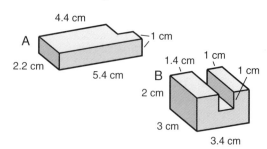

  a) Calculate the volume of prism A.

  c) Calculate the volume of prism B.

B2 a) The area of the grey face of the prism is 16 cm². The volume of the prism is 112 cm³. Calculate the length.

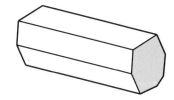

  b) A hexagonal prism is 18 cm long and has a volume of 99 cm³. What is the area of each hexagonal face?

B3 a) Calculate the volume of the wedge.

  b) The cross section of another wedge is a right-angled isosceles triangle with two sides 8 cm long. Its volume is 96 cm³. How long is the wedge?

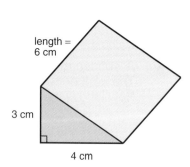

B4 a) Calculate the volume of the cylinder, correct to the nearest 1 cm³.

  b) The volume of a cylinder is 300 cm³. The area of a circular face is 60 cm². What is the height of the cylinder?

B5 Fred Nash has his initials cast in brass. The drawing shows the initials drawn on 1 cm squared paper.
Each brass letter is a prism, 1.5 cm thick.

Calculate the volume of brass used for

  a) the letter F

  b) the letter N.

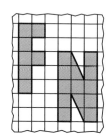

Ma3 LD2 PoS1-2 CHECKER A (LD)

LD2   They calculate lengths, areas and volumes in plane shapes and right prisms.
PoS1-2 Length, area and volume.

Useful formulae

Perimeter of a circle $= \pi \times$ diameter
Area of a circle $= \pi \times$ radius^2
Area of a triangle $= \frac{1}{2} \times$ base length $\times$ height
Volume of a prism $=$ base area $\times$ height
Volume of a cylinder $= \pi \times$ radius$^2 \times$ height

A1 Calculate the area of

a) shape A

b) shape B.

A2 Calculate, correct to the nearest 0.1 cm, the perimeter of

a) shape P

b) shape Q.

A3 a) Calculate the volume of the cylinder, correct to the nearest 1 cm^3.

b) Look at the list of cylinders. Which has the largest volume, A, B or C ?

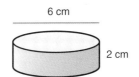

Cylinders
A Radius 5 cm; height 3 cm
B Radius 4 cm; height 5 cm
C Radius 3 cm; height 7 cm

A4 Look at the trapezium. Calculate the area of

a) triangle ABC

b) trapezium ABCD.

A5 a) Prism A has a volume of 900 cm^3. Its length is 15 cm. What is the area of the grey face?

b) The volume of prism B is 70 cm^3. The area of the grey face is 14 cm^2. Calculate the length.

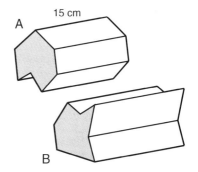

Ma3 █ LD2 █ PoS1-2 █ CHECKER B (LD)

LD2 █ They calculate lengths, areas and volumes in plane shapes and right prisms.
PoS1-2 █ Length, area and volume.

Useful formulae

Perimeter of a circle $= \pi \times$ diameter
Area of a circle $= \pi \times$ radius^2
Area of a triangle $= \frac{1}{2} \times$ base length $\times$ height
Volume of a prism $=$ base area $\times$ height
Volume of a cylinder $= \pi \times$ radius$^2 \times$ height

B1 The shape is made by cutting a 3.2 cm
square from a 6.4 × 5.2 cm rectangle.

Calculate

a) the area of the shape

b) the perimeter of the shape.

B2 PQRS is a rhombus.
SQ = 16 cm.
PR = 12 cm.

Calculate

a) the area of the rhombus

b) the perimeter of the rhombus.

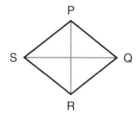

B3 a) Calculate the
volume of the
cylinder, correct
to the nearest
1 cm^3.

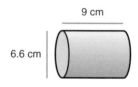

b) Look at the list
of cylinders.
Which has the
largest volume,
P, Q or R?

> **Cylinders**
> P   Radius 1 cm; height 3 cm
> Q   Radius 2 cm; height 2 cm
> R   Radius 3 cm; height 1 cm

B4 The drawing shows a triangular
prism and its end view.

Calculate

a) the area of the end view

b) the volume of the prism.

end view

B5 a) The prism is 4 cm tall.
Its volume is 180 cm^3.
What is the area of the
grey face?

b) The area of each face
of a cube is 25 cm^2.
What is the volume of
the cube?

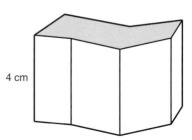

Ma3 LD3 PoS1 CHECKER A (PoS/LD)

LD3   Pupils enlarge shapes by a fractional scale factor.
PoS1   Enlarging shapes.

You need squared paper for Q2 and Q5.

A1 a) Triangle B is an enlargement of triangle A. What is the enlargement scale factor?

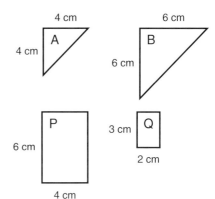

b) Rectangle Q is an enlargement of rectangle P. What is the enlargement scale factor?

A2 *Use squared paper.*
a) Copy and complete the enlargement of the grey shape.

b) What is the enlargement scale factor?

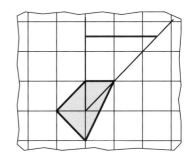

A3 A(1, 1); B (9, 5); C(9, 9) is a triangle. It is enlarged with centre of enlargement at (0, 0) and with scale factor × 4.2.

What are the coordinates of the image of

a) vertex A   b) vertex B ?

A4 A rectangle is enlarged with scale factor × 0.8. The dimensions of the enlarged rectangle are: length 16 cm; width 8 cm.

Calculate the original rectangle's

a) length   b) width.

A5 *Use squared paper.*
Copy the shape. Enlarge it with

a) scale factor × $2\frac{1}{2}$ and centre P

b) scale factor × $3\frac{1}{2}$ and centre Q.

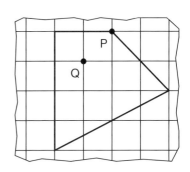

Ma3 ▌ LD3 ▌ PoS1 ▌ CHECKER B (PoS/LD)

LD3 ▪ Pupils enlarge shapes by a fractional scale factor.
PoS1 ▪ Enlarging shapes.

You need squared paper for Q2 and Q5.

B1 a) A square with sides 16 cm long is enlarged with
scale factor × 0.5.
What are the lengths of sides of the image square?

b) An equilateral triangle with sides 10 cm long is
enlarged with scale factor × 1.2.
What are the lengths of sides of the image triangle?

B2 *Use squared paper.*

a) Copy and
complete the
enlargement
of the grey
shape.

b) What is the
enlargement
scale factor?

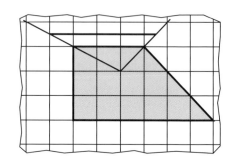

B3 a) Shape B is an
enlargement
of shape A.
What is the
enlargement
scale factor?

b) Rectangle Q is
an enlargement
of rectangle P.
What is X ?

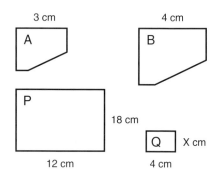

B4 Look at triangle A´B´C´.
It is the image of a triangle
ABC after enlargement
with scale factor × 3.5.

Calculate

a) the length of AB

b) the length of BC.

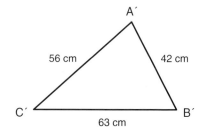

B5 *Use squared paper.*
Copy the shape.
Enlarge it with

a) scale factor × 0.8
and centre L

b) scale factor × 2.5
and centre M.

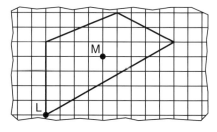

You need squared paper for Q4 and Q5.

A1 A point moves so that its distance
from the *x* axis is always 2 units
greater than its distance from the
y axis.

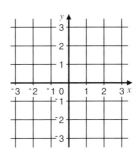

   a) Write down the coordinates
       of one point on its locus.

   b) Write down the coordinates
       of another point on its locus.

A2 A point P moves so that its distance from
a fixed point Q is never more than 3 cm.

    Describe accurately the shape of the
space which P can occupy if it moves

   a) in 2-D   b) in 3-D.

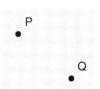

A3 Look at the diagram.
We can describe the locus
of P like this:

    'P moves so that its distance
from B is always three times
its distance from A'.

   a) Describe the locus of Q
       in the same way.

   b) Describe the locus of R
       in the same way.

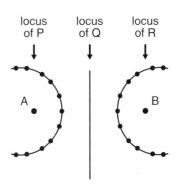

A4 *Use squared paper.*
Copy the grid.

   a) The locus of a point P is given
       by the rule $x + y = 4$.
       Show the path of P on the grid.

   b) The locus of a point Q is given
       by the rule $2x = y$.
       Show the path of Q on the grid.

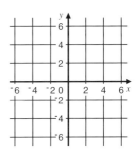

A5 *Use squared paper.*
   a) Copy the diagram.
       Show by shading the locus of a point
       which moves so that its distance from
       A is larger than 1 unit.

   b) Make another copy of the diagram.
       Show by shading the locus of a point
       which moves so that its distance from
       line AB is aways less than 1 unit.

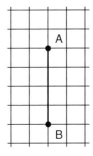

Ma3 LD4 PoS1 CHECKER B (PoS/LD)

LD4 — They determine the locus of an object moving according to a rule.
PoS1 — Locus.

You need squared paper for Q4 and Q5.

B1 A point N moves so that its distance from a fixed point T is exactly 3 cm.

Describe accurately the shape of the space which N can occupy if it moves

a) in 2-D   b) in 3-D.

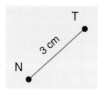

B2 Look at the grid.

a) Write down the equation of the locus of P.

b) Write down the equation of the locus of Q.

locus of P

locus of Q

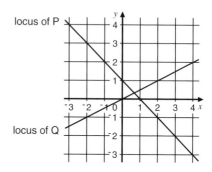

B3 Draw two points M and N 4 cm apart.

a) A point P moves so that its distance from M is twice its distance from N.
Mark 3 points, A, B and C, on the locus of P.

b) A point Q moves so that the sum of its distances from M and from N is always 6 cm.
Mark 3 points, X, Y and Z, on the locus of Q.

B4 *Use squared paper.*
Copy the grid.

a) The locus of a point P is given by the rule $x = y$.
Show the path of P on the grid.

b) The locus of a point Q is given by the rule $x = y - 2$.
Show the path of Q on the grid.

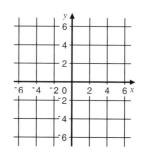

B5 *Use squared paper.*

a) Copy the diagram.
On it show the locus of a point N which moves so that its distance from line E is equal to its distance from line F.

b) Make another copy of the diagram.
On it show the locus of a point K which moves so that its distance from line F is always three times its distance from line E.

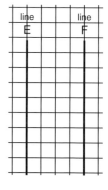

Ma3 ■ LD5 ■ PoS1 ■ CHECKER A (PoS/LD)

LD5 ■ Pupils appreciate the continuous nature of measurement and recognise that a measurement given to the nearest whole number may be inaccurate by up to one half in either direction.

PoS1 ■ Accuracy in measurements.

A1 George measures a line as 4 cm, correct to the nearest cm.

Copy then complete for George's measurement:

a) ...... cm ≤ line length

b) line length < ...... cm.

A2 Malina weighs a bag of sugar. Its mass is 3 kg, correct to the nearest kg.

What is

a) the largest amount of sugar there might be?

b) the least amount of sugar there might be?

SUGAR
3 kg

A3 Alan measures the length of side of a square lawn as 5 m to the nearest metre.

He calculates the perimeter like this:
4×5 m $= 20$ m.

a) How many metres too large might his result be?

b) How many metres too small might his result be?

A4 The distance between two village ponds is measured as 3.8 km, correct to the nearest 0.1 km.

Copy then complete:

a) distance between the ponds < ...... km

b) ...... km ≤ distance between the ponds.

CITY OF PORTSMOUTH
BOYS' SCHOOL
LONDON ROAD, HILSEA
PORTSMOUTH PO2 9RJ
TEL 0705 693521
FAX 0705 665720

A5 Write each approximation like this:
'...... g, correct to the nearest ......'.

a) 57.5 g ≤ mass of a letter < 58.5 g

b) 17.55 g ≤ mass of a postcard < 17.65 g

Ma3 LD5 PoS1 CHECKER B (PoS/LD)

LD5 — Pupils appreciate the continuous nature of measurement and recognise that a measurement given to the nearest whole number may be inaccurate by up to one half in either direction.

PoS1 — Accuracy in measurements.

B1 The sentences in parts a) and b) give an approximation for the lengths of the lines, correct to the nearest cm.

Copy then complete each sentence.

a) Line A: ...... cm ≤ length < ...... cm

b) Line B: ...... cm ≤ length < ...... cm

B2 Eleanor measures out 3 litres of milk, correct to the nearest litre.

What is

a) the largest amount of milk there might be?

b) the least amount of milk there might be?

B3 Write each approximation like this:
'...... km, correct to the nearest ......'.

a) 32.5 km ≤ distance travelled < 33.5 km

b) 19.05 km ≤ distance travelled < 19.15 km

B4 The mass of a marrow is given as 5 kg, correct to the nearest kilogram.

Copy then complete:

a) mass < ...... kg

b) ...... kg ≤ mass.

B5 Keresh weighs three stones. He finds the mass of each stone correct to the nearest 0.1 kg:
2.2 kg, 1.8 kg, 3.3 kg.

a) What is the largest possible total mass of the three stones?

b) What is the smallest possible total mass of the three stones?

Ma3 ▮ LD6 ▮ PoS1 ▮ CHECKER A (PoS)

LD6 ▮ They understand and use compound measures, such as speed.
PoS1 ▮ Distance, speed and time.

A1 Liz walks 120 m at a steady speed.
It takes her 40 seconds.

a) What is her speed, in m/s ?

b) How long will it take her to walk another 60 m ?

A2 The average speed of a train between two railway stations is 60 km/h.
The train takes 2 hours to complete the journey.

a) How far apart are the stations?

b) How long would the same journey take at an average speed of 40 km/h ?

A3 A cross-country race is 8 km long.
The winner's average speed is 16 km/h.

a) What is the winner's time, in minutes?

b) The average speed of the athlete in 2nd place is 15 km/h.
What is this athlete's time, in minutes?

A4 a) A milk float is travelling at 12 km/h.
Write this speed in m/s, correct to 1DP.

b) An aeroplane is flying at 400 m/s.
Write this speed in km/h.

A5 The graph is for the journey of a lorry, starting at 09.00 and ending at 12 noon.

What was the average speed of the lorry

a) for the whole journey

b) during the first 2 hours ?

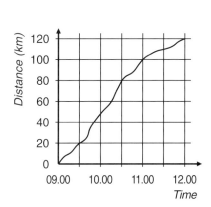

Ma3 ▮ LD6 ▮ PoS2 ▮ CHECKER B (PoS)

LD6 ▮ They understand and use compound measures, such as speed.
PoS2 ▮ Distance, speed and time.

B1 Solomon runs 100 m in 10 seconds.

    a) What is his average speed, in m/s ?

    b) How long would it take Solomon to run 120 m at the same average speed?

B2 A snail travels at a steady speed of 3 cm per min.

  How far does the snail travel

    a) in 5 mins

    b) in 30 secs ?

B3 A van travels 20 km at an average speed of 28 km/h.

  How long does the journey take

    a) correct to the nearest minute

    b) correct to the nearest 10 secs ?

B4 a) A moving pavement carries pedestrians at a steady speed of 3.5 m/s.

      What is this in km/h ?

    b) A bus is travelling at 40 km/h.

      Write this speed in m/s, correct to 1 DP.

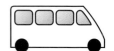

B5 The graph is for the distance fallen by a stone, which is dropped down a well.

  Find the average speed of the stone, in m/s,

    a) during the first 2 seconds

    b) during the next second.

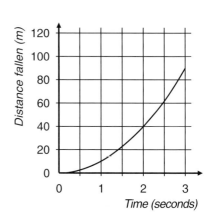

Ma3 ▌LD6 ▌PoS2 ▌CHECKER A (PoS/LD)

LD6 ▎They understand and use compound measures, such as speed.
PoS2 ▎Compound measures.

A1 a) A block of wood has
a volume of 500 cm³,
and a mass of 450 g.
Calculate the density.

b) The density of a metal
rod of volume 400 cm³
is 2.4 g/cm³.
Calculate the mass.

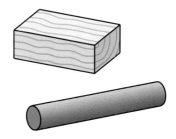

A2 A cog in a machine rotates at
600 revs/min.

a) How many revolutions is
this per hour?

b) How many times does the
cog turn in 20 seconds?

A3 a) The tide is coming in at the
rate of 2.5 m every 4 minutes.
What speed is this in km/h ?

b) The lava from a volcano is
moving at the rate of 300 cm/h.
How many km/day is this?

A4 Acceleration is the rate of increase of speed.
So 4 cm/s² means an increase in speed of
4 cm/s every second.

When a stone is dropped, its acceleration is
approximately 9.8 cm/s².

Approximately, what is the speed of the stone
after

a) 1 second

b) 2 seconds?

A5 a) Calculate the density of the
cube of chocolate.

b) The density of the glass used
to make a marble is 3.5 g/cm³.
Write down a possible mass
and volume for the marble.

2 cm

10 g

Ma3 ▮ LD6 ▮ PoS2 ▮ CHECKER B (PoS/LD)

LD6 ▮ They understand and use compound measures, such as speed.
PoS2 ▮ Compound measures.

B1 a) A plastic toy has a volume of 200 cm^3 and a mass of 210 g. Calculate its density.

b) The density of a block of ice of volume 20 cm^3 is 0.99 g/cm^3. Calculate its mass.

B2 a) Whilst he is asleep, Rover's heart beats at the rate of 72 beats per min. Rover sleeps for 4 hours. How many times does his heart beat?

b) During his walk, Rover's heart beats 1176 times, at an average rate of 84 beats per min. How many minutes long is his walk?

B3 a) A ferry boat takes 8 minutes to cross a river, 400 m wide. What is the average speed of the ferry boat in km/h ?

b) Grass begins to grow on a new lawn at the rate of 0.2 mm/h. At this rate, how long will the grass be, in cm, after 3 days?

B4 a) A sky diver, falling at 20 m/s, opens her parachute and decelerates at an average rate of 4 m/s per second. What is her speed after 2 more seconds?

b) A cyclist decelerates from 30 km/h to 20 km/h in 2 seconds. What is the rate of deceleration in km/h per second ?

B5 a) The oven chip has a 1 cm square cross-section, and a mass of 11 g. Calculate its density.

b) The density of a pebble is 3 g/cm^3. Write down a possible mass and volume for the pebble.

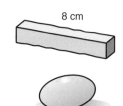

8 cm

Ma4 ▪ LD1 ▪ PoS1 ▪ CHECKER A (PoS/LD)

LD1 ▪ Pupils specify hypotheses and test them by designing and using appropriate methods that take account of bias.
PoS1 ▪ Making hypotheses.

A1 Carla writes this hypothesis:
Smaller families tend to spend more per person on food than do larger families.

   a) Write a question which you might include in a questionnaire to help test Carla's hypothesis.

   b) Write another question.

A2 Sunita is testing this hypothesis:
People in my town visit the cinema more often than they visit the theatre.

These are three samples of people she might consider questioning in order to test her hypothesis:
A   200 people in theatre queues
B   200 people doing Saturday shopping
C   200 students in Sunita's school.

   a) Which sample do you think she should choose?

   b) Choose one of the other samples.
Explain why you think she should not choose this.

A3 George is testing this hypothesis:
Most apples on my tree have a mass less than 140 g.

   a) He collects a representative sample of apples.
He decides to calculate one of these to test his hypothesis:
the range;   the mean;   the median;   the mode.
Which one do you think he should choose?

   b) Explain your choice in part a).

A4 The table shows the prices of some holidays at hotels in Athens and Cairo.

Holiday period	Athens	Cairo
7 days	£380	£360
7 days	£345	£340
10 days	£417	£416
10 days	£427	£422
14 days	£580	£570
14 days	£564	£540

   a) Study the data carefully. Suggest an hypothesis about the relative prices of holidays in the two cities.

   b) What additional information would you collect before you tested the hypothesis?

A5 a) Does the data in Q4 support this hypothesis?
14-day holidays in Athens are more than 30 % cheaper per day than 7-day holidays.
Explain how you decided.

   b) Write a hypothesis about the cost of 7-day and 10-day holidays in Cairo which is supported by the data.
Explain why you think it is supported by the data.

Ma4 █ LD1 █ PoS1 █ CHECKER B (PoS/LD)

LD1   █ Pupils specify hypotheses and test them by designing and using appropriate methods that take account of bias.
PoS1 █ Making hypotheses.

B1   Misha writes this hypothesis:
People over 50 years old are more likely to drink
black coffee than white coffee.

    a)   Write a question which you might include in
        a questionnaire to help test Misha's hypothesis.

    b)   Write another question.

B2   Albert is testing this hypothesis:
More people in my town buy The Times than buy The Mirror.

These are three samples of people that Albert might
question in order to obtain data to test his hypothesis:
A   200 students in his school
B   200 people at the Labour Party meeting
C   200 people at the railway station

    a)   Which sample do you think he should choose?

    b)   Choose one of the other samples.
        Explain why you think he should not choose this.

B3   George wants to test this hypothesis:
Snowdrops flower more quickly when planted 3 cm deep
than when planted 6 cm deep.

He plants two snowdrop bulbs, one 3 cm deep in the
front garden, and one 6 cm deep in the back garden.

    a)   Give one reason why this will not provide a good
        test of the hypothesis.

    b)   Give another reason.

B4   The table shows the times and
distances for some Stop train
and Express train journeys in
Holland and in France.

    a)   Write an hypothesis about
        the relative journey times
        in the two countries.

    b)   What additional information
        would you collect before
        you tested the hypothesis?

	Stop or Express	Distance (km)	Time (mins)
HOLLAND	S	20	25
	S	44	50
	E	55	30
	E	77	39
FRANCE	S	30	56
	S	50	80
	E	60	34
	E	68	39

B5   a)   Does the data in Q4 support this hypothesis?
        Stop train journey times in France are about 3 times longer
        than the equivalent Express train journey times.
        Show how you decided.

      b)   Write an hypothesis about journey times for Stop and
        Express trains in Holland.
        Say whether or not the data in the table supports your
        hypothesis, and explain why.

Ma4 ▮ LD2 ▮ PoS1 ▮ CHECKER A (PoS)

LD2 ▮ They determine the modal class and estimate the mean, median and range of sets of grouped
data, selecting the statistic most appropriate to their line of enquiry.
PoS1 ▮ Mode, range, mean and median for grouped data.

A1 The table gives the masses of 49 goldfish.

Mass (*m* grams)	Number of goldfish
$0 \le m < 20$	21
$20 \le m < 40$	16
$40 \le m < 60$	12

    a) Write down the modal class.

    b) Estimate the range.

A2 a) Mike estimates the mean mass in Q1, using the mid-value of each class interval for his calculation. Do you think his result is less than 30 g, exactly 30 g, or greater than 30 g ?

    b) In which class interval is the median mass in Q1 ?

A3 The frequency diagram gives the heights of the children in a dancing class.

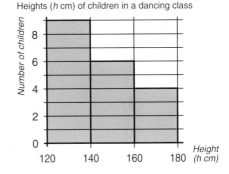

Heights (*h* cm) of children in a dancing class

    a) Write down the modal class.

    b) Estimate the range.

A4 For the data in Q3, estimate these (round each of your results to the nearest 1 cm):

    a) the mean height

    b) the median height.

A5 The frequency diagrams show the number and size of truffles found by the members of two truffle-hunting teams.

[You might not need to calculate to answer a) and b).]

Which team's truffles are more likely to have

    a) the larger mean mass

    b) the larger median mass?

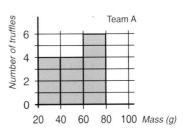

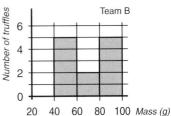

Ma4 ▌LD2 ▌PoS1 ▌CHECKER B (PoS)

LD2 ▌ They determine the modal class and estimate the mean, median and range of sets of grouped
data, selecting the statistic most appropriate to their line of enquiry.
PoS1 ▌ Mode, range, mean and median for grouped data.

B1 The table gives the best
times for running 400 m
for 19 young athletes.

a) Write down the modal
class.

b) Estimate the range.

Time (t seconds)	Number of athletes
$50 \le t < 55$	3
$55 \le t < 60$	7
$60 \le t < 65$	9

B2 a) Karen estimates the mean time in Q1, using the
mid-value of each class interval for her calculation.
Do you think her result is less than 57.5 seconds,
exactly 57.5 seconds, or greater than 57.5 seconds ?

b) In which class interval is the median time in Q1 ?

B3 The frequency
diagram gives
the heights of
31 Christmas
trees.

a) Write down
the modal
class.

b) Estimate
the range.

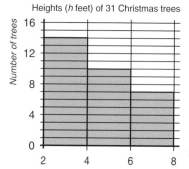

Heights (h feet) of 31 Christmas trees

B4 For the data in Q3, estimate these (round each
of your results to the nearest 0.1 ft):

a) the mean height of the Christmas trees

b) the median height of the Christmas trees.

B5 The frequency diagrams
show the amount of rain
each month in two cities
for a period of 1 year.

[You might not need
to calculate to answer
a) and b).]

Which city do the diagrams
suggest

a) has the larger median
rainfall per month

b) has the larger mean
rainfall per month?

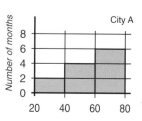

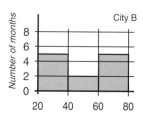

Ma4 LD2 PoS2 CHECKER A (PoS/LD)

LD2 ▪ They determine the modal class and estimate the mean, median and range of sets of grouped data, selecting the statistic most appropriate to their line of enquiry.

PoS2 ▪ Using grouped data.

A1 The table gives the masses of beetroot in a bag (Bag A).

Beetroot in Bag A

Mass (m grams)	Number of beetroot
$30 \leq m < 50$	12
$50 \leq m < 70$	7
$70 \leq m < 90$	5

a) Would you say that the bag contains mainly baby beetroot or mainly mature beetroot? Explain your answer.

b) The bag is either a 1 kg bag or a 1.5 kg bag. Which is more likely? Explain your answer.

A2 The table shows the contents of another bag of beetroot (Bag B).

Beetroot in Bag B

Mass (m grams)	Number of beetroot
$0 \leq m < 40$	12
$40 \leq m < 80$	5
$80 \leq m < 120$	2

a) George says that bag B must have a beetroot heavier than all of those in bag A. Explain why he is wrong.

b) Estimate the mean mass of the beetroots in Bag B. Round your result to the nearest 5 g.

A3 The frequency diagram gives the heights of a group of 11 children.

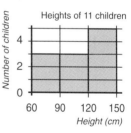

Heights of 11 children

a) Which of A and B do you think is more likely to be the group?
   A 4-year olds at a nursery school
   B Children living in the same street

Explain your choice.

b) Sketch a frequency diagram which you think would fit the group that you rejected in part a).

A4 The children in Q3 visit a model village.

a) 3 children cannot see over the window sills of the houses to look into the rooms. How high above the ground do you think the window sills are? Explain your answer.

b) 5 children can walk through the doors without bending their heads. How tall do you think the doors are? Explain your answer.

A5 Compare these two sets of marks for the same group of 21 students:

21 Students' marks on two tests

Marks	Test 1	Test 2
1 - 5	4	9
6 - 10	10	4
11 - 15	2	5
16 - 20	5	3

a) How many more students scored 10 or more in Test 2 than in Test 1 ?

b) Which Test do you think was more difficult? Why?

Ma4 LD2 PoS2 CHECKER B (PoS/LD)

LD2   They determine the modal class and estimate the mean, median and range of sets of grouped
data, selecting the statistic most appropriate to their line of enquiry.

PoS2   Using grouped data.

B1 The table gives the heights of 19 applicants for a modelling job. The fashion house considers that only 16 of the models are tall enough.

Height (h cm)	Number of applicants
150 ≤ h < 160	6
160 ≤ h < 170	6
170 ≤ h < 180	5
180 ≤ h < 190	2

  a) What do you think is the minimum height required?

  b) Estimate how many applicants are 165 cm tall or taller. Show how you make your estimate.

B2 The diagram shows the ages of the drivers involved in accidents in a town last year.

  a) The local newspaper wants to quote an average age. Which age would you suggest is estimated, the median or the mean? Why?

  b) Write down the modal class.

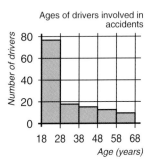

Ages of drivers involved in accidents

B3 The two frequency tables give the number of goals scored by two hockey teams.

Twyford Stars

Goals scored	Number of games
0 - 3	5
4 - 7	11
8 - 11	1

Hove Town

Goals scored	Number of games
0 - 2	5
3 - 5	9
6 - 8	3

  a) In how many games did Twyford score more than 7 goals?

  b) Estimate the number of games in which Hove scored 3 goals or less.

B4 Use the frequency diagrams for Q3.

  a) Estimate the mean number of goals per game for Hove. Round your result to 2 SF and explain how you made the estimate.

  b) Which team do you think is more likely to score more than 3 goals in the next game? Explain your answer.

B5 Compare the numbers of eggs layed by the chickens eating Feed 1 and Feed 2.

Eggs layed in July by 2 sets of chickens

Number of eggs	Feed 1	Feed 2
0 - 4	2	2
5 - 9	10	14
10 - 14	8	7
15 - 19	1	6

  a) Estimate the median number of eggs for Feed 1.

  b) Which Feed do you think is more successful? Why?

Ma4 ▌ LD3 ▌ PoS1 ▌ CHECKER A (PoS/LD)

LD3 ▌ They use measures of average and range, with associated frequency polygons, as appropriate, to compare distributions and make inferences.

PoS1 ▌ Frequency polygons.

A1 Look at the frequency polygon.

a) Roughly how many Caxton kettles were sold between the 12th and 16th week?

b) The sales trend continued. How many kettles do you think were sold between the 24th and 28th week, 500, 650 or 1000 ?

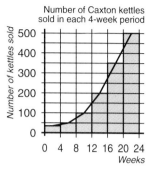

Number of Caxton kettles sold in each 4-week period

A2 The table gives the number of adult men in a town with heights between 160 cm and 200 cm.

a) Draw a frequency polygon for the data in the table.

b) Roughly, how many adult men in the town would you expect to be between 200 and 210 cm tall: 2500, 4500 or 6500 ?

Height (h cm)	Number of men
$160 \leq h < 170$	3000
$170 \leq h < 180$	5500
$180 \leq h < 190$	8000
$190 \leq h < 200$	4500

A3 The two frequency polygons give the masses of the rabbits in two warrens.

a) How many rabbits in Warren A have a mass of less than 1 kg ?

b) Which warren has more rabbits with a mass of less than 1 kg ?

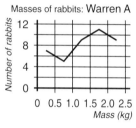

Masses of rabbits: Warren A

A4 Use the frequency polygons in Q3.

a) Estimate the mean mass of the rabbits in Warren A (round your result to the nearest 0.1 kg).

b) Which Warren's rabbits have the larger mean mass?

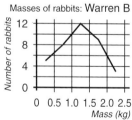

Masses of rabbits: Warren B

A5 The diagram shows two frequency polygons.

a) Look at the frequency polygon for *January*. Is its *shape* what you would expect? Explain your answer.

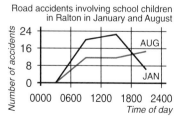

Road accidents involving school children in Ralton in January and August

b) The two frequency polygons have a different *shape*. Describe the main difference *in shape* and say why you think this might be.

Ma4 LD3 PoS1 CHECKER B (PoS/LD)

LD3   ■ They use measures of average and range, with associated frequency polygons, as appropriate, to compare distributions and make inferences.

PoS1   ■ Frequency polygons.

B1 Look at the frequency polygon. Roughly how many trees

    a) were infected between the 18th and 24th month

    b) would you expect to be infected between the 36th and 44th month, if the trend continues?

Dutch elm disease: trees infected in Wark Wood per 6-month interval

B2 The table gives the number of adult women in a town whose mass is between 40 kg and 60 kg.

    a) Draw a frequency polygon for the data in the table.

    b) Roughly, how many adult women in the town would you expect to have a mass between 60 and 65 kg: 1000, 2000 or 3000 ?

Mass (m kg)	Number of women
$40 \leq m < 45$	1300
$45 \leq m < 50$	4800
$50 \leq m < 55$	5200
$55 \leq m < 60$	2100

B3 The two frequency polygons give the number of days on which less than 10 mm of rain fell in two cities during 1980.

    a) Roughly, how many of the days in City A had less than 10 mm of rain?

    b) Which city had the greater number of days with less than 10 mm of rain?

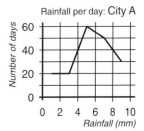

Rainfall per day: City A

B4 Use the frequency polygons in Q3.

Make these estimates for the days recorded in the diagrams (round your results to the nearest mm):

    a) the mean amount of rain per day in City A

    b) the median amount of rain per day in city B.

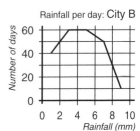

Rainfall per day: City B

B5 The scores on the two Science tests are for the same pupils.

    a) The pass mark for each test was 10. How many pupils passed Test 1 ?

    b) Which test would you say was more difficult? Explain your answer.

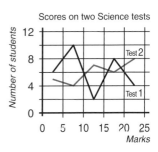

Scores on two Science tests

Ma4 ▌LD4 ▌PoS1 ▌CHECKER A (PoS/LD)

LD4 ▪ They draw a line of best fit on a scatter diagram, by inspection.
PoS1 ▪ Lines of best fit.

You need squared paper for Q4.

A1 Look at the scatter diagram.
It shows the lengths and
masses of 12 trout.

a) Which line, A or B, is
the line of best fit?

b) Estimate the mass of
a 22 cm trout.

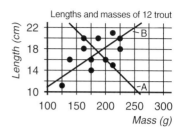
Lengths and masses of 12 trout

A2 Look at the scatter diagram.
It shows the number of steps
taken by people of different
heights, in walking 100 m.

a) Which line, P or Q, is
the line of best fit?

b) Estimate how many
steps a 220 cm tall
person would take.

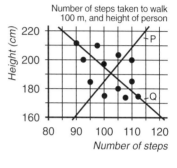
Number of steps taken to walk
100 m, and height of person

A3 The scatter diagram shows
the masses of some cast
iron saucepans and their lids.

a) Which line, L or M, is the
line of best fit?

b) Another cast iron saucepan
has a mass of 1200 g.
Estimate the mass of its lid.

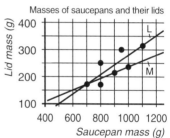
Masses of saucepans and their lids

A4 *Use squared paper.*

a) Copy the scatter diagram.
Draw the line of best fit.
Label it J.

b) Plot these two additional
points: (12 years, 16 CDs),
(14 years, 12 CDs).
Draw the new line of best
fit. Label it K.

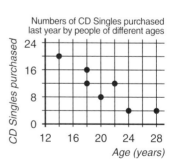
Numbers of CD Singles purchased
last year by people of different ages

A5 The scatter diagram shows the
times taken by mountaineers
to reach a base camp when
carrying different loads.

a) Predict the time taken for
a load of 25 kg.

b) Predict the load carried
for a time of 44 minutes.

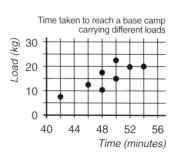
Time taken to reach a base camp
carrying different loads

Ma4 ▪ LD4 ▪ PoS1 ▪ CHECKER B (PoS/LD)

LD4 ▪ They draw a line of best fit on a scatter diagram, by inspection.
PoS1 ▪ Lines of best fit.

You need squared paper for Q4.

B1 Look at the scatter diagram. It shows the heights of 12 sunflowers and the widths of their flower heads.

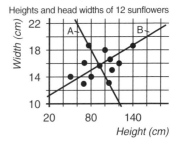

Heights and head widths of 12 sunflowers

a) Which line, A or B, is the line of best fit?

b) Estimate the head width of a 160 cm tall sunflower.

B2 Look at the scatter diagram. It shows the number of hours of training of some dogs for the blind, and the number of errors they make in a test.

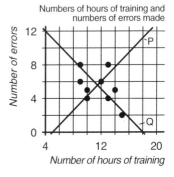

Numbers of hours of training and numbers of errors made

a) Which line, P or Q, is the line of best fit?

b) Estimate the number of hours training needed before no errors are made.

B3 Look at the scatter diagram. It shows the lengths and widths of some leaves, all from the same tree.

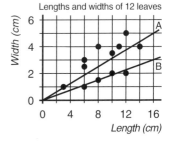

Lengths and widths of 12 leaves

a) Which line, A or B, is the line of best fit?

b) Another leaf is 16 cm long. Estimate its width.

B4 *Use squared paper.*

Goals scored and goals conceded by 7 hockey teams

a) Copy the scatter diagram. Draw the line of best fit. Label it K.

b) Plot these two extra points: (24 scored, 0 conceded), (26 scored, 4 conceded). Draw the new line of best fit. Label it L.

B5 The scatter diagram shows times taken to raise marble blocks onto a roof using a pulley system.

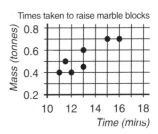

Times taken to raise marble blocks

a) Predict the time taken for a block of mass 0.8 tonnes.

b) Predict the mass of a block that takes 14 minutes to raise.

Ma4 LD5 PoS1 CHECKER A (PoS/LD)

LD5   Pupils understand relative frequency as an estimate of probability and use this to compare outcomes of experiments.

PoS1   Relative frequency.

A1 There are 2000 small coloured beads in the jar.
Mike takes out a sample of 50.
25 are red and 14 are blue.

What is the relative frequency

a) of red beads

b) of blue beads?

2000 BEADS

A2 Tariq spins a spinner a large number of times.
The possible outcomes are RED, GREEN, BLUE.
The table shows the results.

RED	GREEN	BLUE
13	28	19

a) What is the relative frequency of RED ?

b) How many times would you expect to score RED in 300 spins?

A3 In a sample of 200 trees from a commercial orchard, 66 are found to have red spot disease.

a) What is the relative frequency of red spot disease?

b) There are 3500 trees in the orchard.
Estimate the number that have red spot disease.

CITY OF PORTSMOUTH
BOYS' SCHOOL
LONDON ROAD, HILSEA
PORTSMOUTH PO2 9RJ
TEL 0705 693521
FAX 0705 665720

A4 In a random sample of cars, the relative frequency of cars with fewer than 4 doors is 0.64.

a) What is the relative frequency of cars with 4 doors or more?

b) In the sample, 32 cars have fewer than 4 doors.
How many cars have 4 doors or more?

A5 The four cards are turned over and shuffled.
Carl then selects a card.
He wins if he chooses D.

The table shows the results for 240 trials.

a) Use the results to calculate the relative frequency of the letter A.

b) Do the results suggest that Carl's choice is random?
Explain your answer.

A	135
D	105

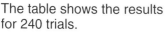

Ma4 LD5 PoS1 CHECKER B (PoS/LD)

LD5 Pupils understand relative frequency as an estimate of probability and use this to compare
outcomes of experiments.

PoS1 Relative frequency.

B1 A random sample of 500 poppy
seeds is taken from a total of
about 12 000 seeds.
480 of the sample are found
to be fertile.

What is the relative frequency

a) of fertile seeds

b) of infertile seeds?

B2 In a random sample of 400 words from
an essay, 236 have exactly two vowels.

a) Estimate the probability that a word
chosen at random has exactly two
vowels.

b) The essay is 4800 words long.
Estimate the number of words in
the essay with exactly two vowels.

B3 A random sample of beads
is taken from a box containing
a large number of white, red
and yellow beads.
The table shows the results.

What is the relative frequency

a) of white beads

b) of red beads?

WHITE	RED	YELLOW
14	23	3

B4 A group of tasters say which of two sandwich spreads
they prefer, X or Y.
The relative frequency of X-preferences is 0.7.

a) What is the relative frequency of Y-preferences?

b) 28 tasters say they prefer X.
How many say they prefer Y ?

B5 In a random sample of 4000 light bulbs,
0.2 % are found to be faulty.

a) Write the relative frequency of faulty
bulbs as a decimal.

b) A supermarket buys 260 bulbs and
finds that 2 are faulty.
Is this more than might have been
expected?
Explain your answer.